the baby

emergency handbook

Lifesaving Information
Every Parent Needs to Know

Lawrence E. Shapiro, Ph.D.
Richard L. Jablow, MD, FA...

D1115683

New Harbinger Public...

Publisher's Note

Distributed in Canada by Raincoast Books

Copyright © 2008 by Lawrence E. Shapiro
New Harbinger Publications, Inc.
5674 Shattuck Avenue
Oakland, CA 94609
www.newharbinger.com

Cover design by Amy Shoup; Illustrations by Julie Olson; Text design by Amy Shoup and Michele Waters-Kermes; Image editing by Sara Christian; Acquired by Tesilya Hanauer; Edited by Karen O'Donnell Stein

All photos are models used for illustrative purposes only.

All Rights Reserved. Printed in China.

Library of Congress Cataloging-in-Publication Data

Shapiro, Lawrence E.
The baby emergency handbook : lifesaving information every parent needs to know / Lawrence E. Shapiro, Richard L. Jablow, and Julia Holmes.
p. cm.
ISBN-13: 978-1-57224-566-2 (pbk. : alk. paper)
ISBN-10: 1-57224-566-2 (pbk. : alk. paper) 1. Pediatric emergencies--Handbooks, manuals, etc. 2. Pediatric emergencies--Popular works. I. Jablow, Richard L. II. Holmes, Julia. III. Title.
RJ370.S488 2008
618.92'0025--dc22

2008013219

10   09   08

10   9   8   7   6   5   4   3   2   1   First printing

To the memory of my mother, Frances Shapiro,
who loved all babies and taught me to do the same
—Lawrence E. Shapiro, Ph.D.

contents

PART 4
Appendices   163

Important Note to the Reader

Please keep all of the following important cautions in mind as you read and use this book!

- As a general rule, call 911 first in cases of emergency. For a discussion of what constitutes an emergency and what to do if you are alone with a baby or child and must choose between calling 911 or immediate intervention with your child, the authors suggest that you become familiar with the contents of this book and contact the American Heart Association for classes.

- Although this book contains information about CPR and other child-rescue techniques, it is meant to be used as a supplement to (and not as a substitute for) a certified course in CPR and child rescue. Please enroll in an approved course today.

- This book describes various approaches to dealing with a number of common emergency situations. However, it is impossible for a single book to cover every possible emergency and every possible approach to handling an emergency. The reader is encouraged to seek out other sources of information and to discuss the handling of health emergencies with your physician.

- The authors and the publisher have used their best efforts to make sure that the contents of this book are correct and consistent with the medical information and techniques that were current at the time of publication. However, such information and techniques may have changed since this edition was published. In any event, this book cannot and does not take the place of advice and treatment from a qualified health-care professional.

- This book is sold without warranties or guarantees of any kind, and the authors and publisher disclaim any responsibility or liability for injuries, losses or damages that may result from the use of the information and advice contained in this book.

foreword

The term "accident" implies that nothing could have been done to prevent an event from occurring. We as parents and physicians will never be able to prevent all accidents from happening. However, we can do a great deal to prevent many accidents from occurring and train ourselves and each other to effectively deal with those accidents that inevitably do happen.

For example, through widespread public education regarding the benefits of seat-belt use, as well as some legislation concerning the same, we have managed to decrease the number of serious injuries from automobile accidents significantly in the last decade. Most adults of a certain age remember when there were no seat belts in automobiles and are likely to tell you that they didn't use them religiously when they were first available. Now, the use of seat belts is so common that many young children will even ask for their seat belt to be fastened. On the other hand, we as a society have only begun to make positive changes with regard to issues such as binge drinking and drunk driving.

During my medical training, my fellow students and I received very little instruction in preventative medicine in any organized fashion. What Dr. Shapiro has given us in his outstanding *Baby Emergency Handbook* is a source rich in both preventative medicine and treatment modalities that we should be aware of, particularly as parents. Prevention is better and perhaps even easier to learn than treatment.

Think about it: when we want to begin driving a car or piloting a boat, we study, practice, even obtain the necessary licensing. So why should we not want to learn and study as much about preventing emergencies in our children? I am here to tell you that accidents happen all the time and across all socioeconomic barriers. Knowing what to do can literally make the difference between life and death for your child.

For example, if your child has a complete airway obstruction from choking on a hot dog, you have three to four minutes to remove the obstruction before irreversible brain damage can begin to occur. You had better know what to do. Looking for this book is not the best answer in that moment. Having read the book ahead of time so you know what to do is. The time to review these is not during a crisis, but before one ever arises.

Similarly, I would strongly encourage anyone who is considering raising a child to seek out and take as many courses as you can from your local

American Heart Association, Red Cross, or hospital. These courses are ubiquitous and reasonably priced. I furthermore tell all parents that they are really not likely to be competent in issues such as airway management or CPR until the American Heart Association has deemed them to be.

I remember what my medical school adviser told me once: books are easy to purchase, somewhat more difficult to read, and most difficult to learn. While it would be impossible to have a single reference book that deals with all childhood emergencies, this book covers many common emergencies and should be considered a valuable reference book in any home.

—Richard Lee Jablow, MD, FACEP

acknowledgments

Some people have asked me why a child psychologist would write a book on medical emergencies. My response is simple: though the emergencies in this book are medical problems for infants and young children, they are psychological problems for their parents. In writing and organizing this book, I have come to realize that highly stressful moments, such as emergency situations, are accompanied by psychological issues, which may prevent a parent from responding in a prompt and helpful way. For this reason, I have asked myself, "What steps can be taken to reduce the psychological stress related to childhood emergencies, thereby helping parents to respond more quickly and effectively when their child is in danger?" The answer is threefold: taking measures to prevent the emergency in the first place, having the advance knowledge of what to do, and being equipped with tools to act quickly and confidently when every moment counts.

That being said, I could not have completed this book without the diligent research of my coauthor, Julia Holmes, and the wisdom and expertise of my other coauthor, Dr. Richard Jablow, an emergency-room physician with more than twenty years' experience. Thank you for all of your work on this important project.

I would also like to thank the supportive staff at New Harbinger Publications, particularly Dr. Matt McKay, Julie Bennett, Tesilya Hanauer, and Julie Kahn. I would also like to acknowledge my personal staff, Elizabeth Kenney, Karen Schader, and Donna Solano, for their unwavering encouragement, and especially for listening to my endless stories and anecdotes.

Finally, I would like to thank all of the parents who have shared their personal stories of baby emergencies. Your insight has guided me during every stage of this project.

Speaking for myself and my coauthors, I would also like to say hello to all the babies whose parents are reading this book. I wish you a long, happy, and healthy life. As you grow, give your parents 100 million kisses for taking such good care of you.

—Lawrence E. Shapiro, Ph.D.
September 2007

PART 1

introduction:
when bad things happen
to good babies

When I began writing this book I asked every parent I knew if they had experienced an emergency when their children were infants. Over 80 percent said yes.

For a friend it was a car accident when her daughter was just three months old. For a colleague it was a fall off the kitchen counter when her infant was just five months old. Another friend told me about her son choking on a piece of hot dog at his first birthday party. I heard stories about food allergies, burns, bee stings, and much more. Fortunately, not one of these children had a permanent injury as a result of the emergency situation.

We have written this book to make sure that, if you are confronted by an emergency with your young child, you will know what to do, and, like in the vast majority of situations, your baby's emergency will soon be just a bad memory. *The Baby Emergency Handbook* was designed so you can always have it with you. Keep it in your diaper bag so wherever your baby goes, the book will go too. In the back of this book you will find important information that you and the other adults who care for your infant need to know, including:

- A fold-out diagram of how to perform infant CPR

- A section on how to identify and relieve choking in infants and children

- A list of national hotlines

- A place to put your own emergency numbers

But don't wait until there is an emergency to read the book! Each section of this book begins with information on how to prevent the problem. Read these sections carefully and have other people who care for your child do the same.

As part of your prevention program, we urge you to also take a course on baby first aid, and in particular infant CPR. These are offered by your local hospital or American Heart Association or Red Cross chapter. There is no substitute for hands-on training when your baby's health and safety are involved.

At the end of each section in this book you will also find suggested issues to think about as your child grows. Unfortunately, emergencies do not end when your baby becomes a more resourceful and independent child, nor even when your child becomes a sturdy, nearly grown-up teen. Your baby will change in many ways over these years, but dangers will persist, as will your concern for your child's safety. And, at every stage, you will find that being prepared and informed is the best way to protect your child.

PART 2

ten ways to get faster help when your baby is in danger

All parents dread the thought of facing an emergency with their baby. Besides the danger to their child and the harm it might inflict, parents are naturally concerned that they might panic, react too slowly, or even inadvertently do the wrong thing.

I hope it calms you to know that the vast majority of parents do *exactly* the right thing in an emergency, acting with speed and assurance. Like parents from other animal species, you are genetically wired to protect your young, and the moment you see that your child is in danger or hurt, your brain produces a powerful chemical potion to make your mind hyperalert, your reflexes superfast, and your problem-solving abilities laser sharp.

You *will* be ready to do the right thing if your baby is in danger, but you will be more ready when armed with the right information. Read the prevention sections in this book thoroughly. As they say, an ounce of prevention is worth a pound of cure. Then go through the five tips on the next few pages to further increase your preparedness and make sure that you are absolutely at your best when every second counts. Check off each tip as you complete it.

Next you'll find five specific things you can do if an emergency happens. These tips will help you be most effective in getting your infant the care he or she needs. You may want to mark this section so that you can turn to it quickly in the event of an emergency.

The most important thing you can do is to keep this book with your baby, as it contains personal information that will aid caretakers and doctors in treating your baby most efficiently and effectively, emergency numbers, and valuable information about common emergencies.

Five Things to Do to Prepare for an Emergency

1. Always Have Emergency Numbers with You

Calling 911 or your local emergency phone number will connect you with your local network of police and fire departments for a quick on-the-scene response. If your baby has been in an automobile accident, is having difficulty breathing, has been burned, or shows other signs of acute distress, it is always appropriate to immediately call 911 or your local emergency number. In situations like this, when it comes to your child's health and safety, overreacting is often better than underrreacting.

But there are times, when your baby is not in acute distress, that other emergency numbers might be helpful. For example, we recommend calling your local poison-control line (even before you call the national hotline) if you suspect that your baby has ingested any nonfood liquid or chemical. Your local poison-control center will usually answer faster than the national hotline, and it is staffed by operators familiar with the dangers in your geographic area.

In the back of the book we have included a list of national hotlines, and also a place for you to write your own emergency numbers, including the numbers of your pediatrician, your local hospital, your close family, and so on. Make sure to fill in this section completely. Give these numbers to anyone taking care of your infant—a day-care center, babysitter, or another adult. You can leave this book with your baby's things. Anyone who cares for your infant will be reassured to know that these numbers are available at all times.

2. Keep Your Baby's Medical Information with You at All Times

In the back of this book you can record your baby's medical history, which might be helpful in case of an emergency. If you keep this book in your diaper bag (as we recommend), then you will be sure to have your baby's medical history when you go to the hospital.

Another option is to keep your family medical history on a small removable computer drive, sometimes called a "thumb drive" or "flash drive." There are a variety of software-and-thumb-drive combinations that let you carry around an enormous amount of important information with you on your key ring, including medical information about your infant and other members of your family. When you get to the hospital, the intake coordinator can just plug your thumb drive into any USB port and instantly have access to your baby's medical records.

3. Establish an Emergency Plan

What would happen if you suddenly became ill? What would happen if you lost electricity in your home in the middle of the night? What would happen if you had a fire in your home or a natural disaster struck?

Parents should enlist family and friends to establish an emergency plan. Make sure that all the people who take care of your infant know where your local emergency room is located and what to do when they get there (see the next group of tips).

4. Visit Your Local Emergency Room

Ask your pediatrician for advice regarding which emergency room he or she might prefer, or contact your insurance company to find out which hospitals are in its network. However, do keep in mind that with some emergencies the closest ER is the best choice.

As soon as you can, take an hour to visit your emergency room, both the one preferred by your pediatrician or insurance company and the one closest to you, preferably *without* your infant or other children (you certainly don't want to bring young children to places where they may encounter airborne diseases, if you can help it). Note where you would park in case of an emergency, where the entrance to the ER is, and where you go to sign in. You might want to pick up any brochures that could be helpful.

Take your time. Sit down and observe what is going on, particularly if there are other parents with young children in the ER. Becoming familiar with the ER when you are calm and not in the throes of your own emergency will make it much easier for you if the need for a real visit arises.

5. Take a Course in Infant and Child CPR

You will hear this advice again and again throughout this book: take a course in infant CPR and first aid *as soon as possible.* Ask other adults who take care of your infant to take this course too.

Courses in CPR are offered by your local hospital and Red Cross and American Heart Association chapters, and are given regularly throughout the year. You might also arrange your own training through a Red Cross or American Heart Association chapter at a time that is convenient for you, bringing an instructor to your place of work or even to a home party. There is a small fee associated with the training, but it is money well spent.

There are several videos that demonstrate CPR with children (for example *Infant & Child CPR* by Tracy Kalemba, produced by Matty Mo Media), but *you should not consider yourself ready to do CPR with children until you have live training.*

When an Emergency Happens to Your Child

1. Determine Whether to Bring Your Child to the ER

Let's say your child has an emergency—perhaps not a life-threatening one, but one that causes you concern. You call your pediatrician and he or she says, "It's okay; bring your child into the office in the morning." If you are not comfortable with that answer, then you may need to make the decision regarding whether to follow the doctor's advice, or bring the child to the ER immediately.

I suggest that if you are concerned, worried, or unwilling to wait, then go to the emergency room. More than once I have seen parents who have saved their child's life because they decided not to wait. Of course, the downside of going to the ER immediately is that you must be prepared to wait for quite a long time, and you may be told that the injury or illness is not serious and that you should see your pediatrician.

2. Be Direct and Honest When You Seek Admission to the ER

If you decide to go to the ER, when you present your baby to the intake worker, state the problem simply and directly. Do not hold anything back. You may be inclined to omit some detail that might make you seem careless or negligent, but it is important that you state exactly what happened to ensure that your infant gets the appropriate treatment.

3. Write Things Down

When checking in at the ER, ask for a piece of paper and a pen if you don't have one. When doctors or other medical personnel give you information about your child, write it down as soon as you have a chance. You may think you will remember what they are saying, but later you may have difficulty remembering important details about your child's illness or the procedures that were performed. Also, write down the names of the doctors who are seeing your child. You can also ask that a copy of your emergency department record be e-mailed to your child's pediatrician.

4. Contact a Trusted Relative or Friend When You Get to the ER

As soon as you are able, call someone you know and trust and tell them what has happened. Choose someone who will be likely to respond calmly in an emergency because you may need him or her to care for your other children, make calls, look up information, and provide support. This person might be your spouse or your own parent, but it might be a neighbor or coworker as well. Think of the one person you can rely on most in an emergency, and who is also likely to be available to help you.

5. Ask Questions and Make Sure You Understand the ER's Discharge Instructions

Emergency rooms can be busy and intimidating places, but you should always ask as many questions as you need to. Many people don't know that some hospitals offer case-management services. If you aren't assigned a case manager, ask to see one. A case worker can be very helpful and reassuring during admittance or transfer to another hospital, or when you're being discharged.

Make sure that you are given clear discharge instructions, read them immediately, and ask questions. Make sure that the ER staff will communicate with your primary physician and follow up with a phone call.

PART 3

the emergencies

Abduction

Avoiding the Problem

Media coverage of child abductions may make you feel that your baby is in imminent danger of being snatched from her stroller or crib. In fact, only a relatively small number of children are abducted each year, and most of these children are taken by a noncustodial parent, not a stranger. Infants are rarely abducted. According to the National Crime Information Center, the rate for abduction increases as children enter elementary school and peaks at age fifteen. Teenage girls are considered most vulnerable.

In most cases of baby abductions, babies are abducted by women who plan to bring up the child as their own. When infant abductions occur, they most often take place in hospitals, nurseries, or other public places.

Precautions should be obvious, but they are still worth mentioning:

- Never leave children alone in a car or stroller, even for a moment.

- Choose caregivers—babysitters, nannies, and day-care centers— carefully and check all references. If caregivers pick children up from school, be sure the school or day-care center is notified of the arrangement.

- Keep your baby's birth certificate or adoption papers in a handy place in case you have to provide proof of parenthood.

What to Do if Your Baby Is Abducted or Missing

Stay calm. It's most important to think clearly and act rationally. Notify the authorities immediately. **Call 911 first.** Then, if you are in a public place, such as a store, **notify store employees or anyone who might have been present when your baby was taken**.

The hours immediately following a kidnapping are critical ones. Cases of child abduction have the best chance of being solved if parents can **provide key information to law enforcement: their child's height, weight, and eye color; a description of what their child was wearing at the time of the abduction; and a recent photo of their child.**

Although most parents have recent photos on hand, surprisingly few are able to remember their child's height, weight, and details of their appearance in the profoundly stressful aftermath of a kidnapping. This is understandable: children change so quickly that it can be hard for parents—who see them every day—to keep track of how much their child has grown and changed.

However, because the first few hours are the most critical in cases of missing children, it's important to have this information immediately available.

The National Center for Missing & Exploited Children provides fact sheets and tips for keeping kids of all ages safe, and help in the event that a child is missing. The hotline is 1-800-THE-LOST (1-800-843-5678), and the website is www.missingkids.com.

As Your Child Grows

As children grow older and spend more time at school, with friends, or with other caregivers, it's important for parents to arm them with as much good stranger sense as possible, without making them fearful of the world around them.

Remind children that they should never go anywhere with an adult they don't know or who makes them feel uncomfortable, regardless of what that adult says. Also tell children they never have to do anything for an adult they don't know. Teach them to scream "No!" and to run away if any adult tries to coerce them to go with them.

Many police departments and schools organize easy and helpful finger-printing programs; it's a good idea to have your child participate in such a program if one is available to you. Keep all medical, dental, and other records up to date. Make sure young children know their names, address, and phone number, and whom to call in an emergency.

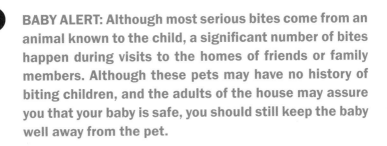

BABY ALERT: Although most serious bites come from an animal known to the child, a significant number of bites happen during visits to the homes of friends or family members. Although these pets may have no history of biting children, and the adults of the house may assure you that your baby is safe, you should still keep the baby well away from the pet.

What to Do if Your Baby Is Bitten by an Animal

If the Wound Is Superficial

Wash the injured area with warm water and soap and rinse the area under running water for five minutes. Then **pat the wound dry** with a sterile cloth or clean cloth diaper, **cover it with antibiotic cream**[*] **and an adhesive bandage**, and **bring your child to his pediatrician or the closest emergency room**. Over the next day or two, look for any possible signs of infection, including redness, pus, or swelling around the wound; sweating, fever, or chills; and swollen glands. If any of these symptoms appear, contact your pediatrician, or go straight to the ER.

---

[*]   Assuming your child is not allergic to the cream

BABY ALERT: A large dog can generate a crush injury without breaking the skin. Early signs would be swelling and bruising. Whenever a child is bitten or knocked down by an animal it is advisable to immediately take your child to your pediatrician or an emergency room.

If the Bite Is Serious and Bleeding, or if the Bite Is on Your Child's Face

Place a clean gauze pad or sterile cloth on the wound and apply direct pressure with your fingers. If the bite is on the arm or hand, continue applying pressure and lift the injured area above the level of your child's heart. **Once the bleeding is under control, cover the wound with clean sterile dressing and take your child to the closest emergency room.** Serious bites will often require stitches.

If the Bite Is from a Wild Animal

Treat the wound exactly as you would a bite from a domesticated animal, and then take your child to the doctor or emergency room. If at all possible, safely **trap the animal or contain it in a fenced area.** Then call the local animal control or health department office listed in your telephone directory (this may also be done by the emergency room staff). The animal control staff can retrieve the animal and have it checked for rabies. If you cannot test the animal, then your child may have to undergo antirabies treatment.

 PARENT SMART: Bites from bats, skunks, foxes, coyotes, raccoons, and wild dogs and cats are the most concerning. Rodents, such as mice, chipmunks, rats, and squirrels, are considered less dangerous; however, always let your ER doctor and pediatrician determine the best course of treatment.

As Your Child Grows

Understandably, young children who are bitten may become wary of animals. Sometimes this fear will be specific to the species that bit him, but it is not uncommon for children to become fearful of many different kinds of animals. Do not force him to approach a pet or other animal, and do not make light of his fear. Over time, most children will forget about the incident, but remember that children's safety around animals should always be a concern.

Asthma

Avoiding the Problem

Asthma is a chronic lung disease that causes airways to become inflamed, leading to coughing, wheezing, and shortness of breath. An estimated 10 to 12 percent of children in the United States have asthma, making it the most common chronic illness in children.

A variety of risk factors can cause asthma, including allergies, a family history of asthma, frequent respiratory infections, low birth weight, and exposure to tobacco smoke before and after birth.

Asthma can be difficult to diagnose in babies since their airways are smaller and more vulnerable to other illnesses that may look like asthma. If your baby has chronic breathing problems, a thorough examination should be done to determine whether asthma is the cause.

It's important to remember this rule of thumb: "All that wheezes is not asthma, and all asthma episodes do not include wheezing." Just one instance of wheezing isn't enough to diagnose asthma, but even recurring wheezing may not be due to asthma (fewer than one third of infants with recurring wheezing in the first three years of life go on to develop asthma). As your baby grows older, more tests will be available to determine whether or not she has this chronic condition.

The simplest treatment for asthma is to avoid asthma triggers. These include exercise (in older children), exposure to strong odors and irritant fumes, smoke, cold air, social stress, anxiety, viruses, air pollution, allergies, and tobacco smoke—which clings to clothing even when the person has been smoking outside.

What to Do if Your Baby Has Asthma

During an asthma attack, your child may wheeze (although if the attack is severe she may not be moving enough air to create wheezing). She may have difficulty breathing, possibly so much that she can't walk or complete a sentence without becoming short of breath. She may sit in a hunched-over, tripodlike position in order to make breathing easier.

In a severe attack, your child's chest muscles may retract, she may breathe abdominally, and she may appear frightened.

Get immediate medical help if you notice any of the following:

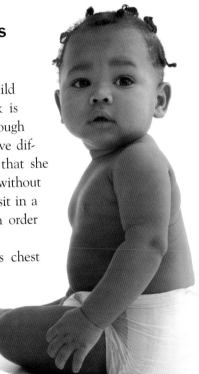

- The baby's breathing is erratic or distressed.

- The baby is retracting her chest muscles—pulling in the ribcage, the area below the breastbone, or the area above the collarbones— in an effort to draw a full breath.

- The baby has bluish coloring, which can indicate respiratory and heart problems.

- The baby is flaring her nostrils repeatedly—this can be a sign that she is trying to draw in needed air.

- The baby makes unusual grunting sounds—he or she may be trying to hold or draw additional oxygen into the lungs and may be struggling to breathe. Moaning while exhaling may also indicate breathing problems.

- The baby is working too hard to breathe.

If your child is having an asthma attack or flare-up, it is important to **follow the steps of your asthma action plan as outlined by your doctor**. You'll need to keep a list of medications that your doctor has recommended or prescribed, and make sure never to leave home without them. If you are concerned about the severity of the attack, **take your child to the emergency room**.

School-age children are often very articulate about their symptoms, and they may be able to tell you whether they are experiencing a bad episode. In infants, asthma is often preceded by a viral illness, runny nose, and tight cough, so be on the watch for these symptoms.

Untreated asthma may damage the lungs over time, so an **early use of anti-inflammatory medications may be recommended**. The more details you can provide medical service providers about your child's symptoms, the more accurate diagnosis and treatment she will receive.

As Your Child Grows

Asthma cannot be cured but it can controlled and managed, allowing the asthmatic child to lead an active, normal life.

Some children may seem to outgrow asthma, but this can be misleading: 50 percent of children with asthma experience a noticeable decrease in symptoms by the time they reach adolescence, but half of the time symptoms will develop again later in life.

Bee Stings

Avoiding the Problem

Bees, wasps, hornets, and yellow jackets generally steer clear of people, but they can be a menace at a picnic or other outing, drawn in by the allure of food, sugary drinks, or even the botanical scents of shampoos. Avoid taking your baby to areas that are likely to be buzzing with bee activity in the summer and early fall: orchards in bloom, flower-filled gardens, public garbage cans, and other sources of nectar and sugar. If you are in an area where you know there are bees, long pants and long sleeves may provide your baby with some protection.

If a bee or wasp flies near you or your baby, don't swat at it! This will only excite its defensive instincts. Just stay still or move very calmly away. Insect repellents have no effect on stinging insects—the best defense is to just stay away.

What to Do if Your Baby Is Stung

A sting can be a painful experience for adults, but babies and children are even more affected by insect venom because of their small size. However, stings should be considered a common occurrence and not cause for alarm (unless an allergic reaction develops).

If a bee is responsible for the sting, you may be able to see the stinger embedded in the skin—**use your fingernail or the edge of a credit card to** *gently* **scrape away the stinger. Do not pull at the stinger with your fingers or tweezers**; this may push more venom into the bloodstream. Although there are debates about the best means of taking out the stinger, there is no dispute that the stinger should be removed right away. Hornets, wasps, and yellow jackets can sting multiple times and do not leave behind a stinger.

In all cases, **wash the swollen area with soap and water and apply a cool cloth or ice pack (or calamine lotion)** to reduce pain and further swelling, both of which should subside after a few hours. Do not apply heat.

PARENT SMART: Depending on your child's age and weight, acetaminophen may be recommended. Call your pediatrician before making this determination, particularly if your child is less than six months of age.

In rare cases, a sting can cause a potentially fatal allergic reaction called anaphylactic shock. This sometimes deadly reaction includes hives, facial swelling, difficulty breathing, marked weakness, vomiting, abdominal cramps, or sleepiness or confusion, the latter being possible indications of shock. Stings by yellow jackets are the most common cause of allergic reactions. If there are any signs of a serious allergic reaction right after the sting or hours afterward, seek immediate medical attention. If your child is stung in the mouth or nose, this may also cause respiratory distress, and you should take your child directly to the ER. Also, go to the ER if a child under one year old has multiple stings.

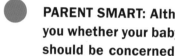 **PARENT SMART: Although there is no test that will tell you whether your baby will be allergic to bee stings, you should be concerned about this problem if you have a family history of allergies to stings, or if your infant has other allergies.**

As Your Child Grows

Teach children about different insects—how they behave and where they make their homes—so children can learn to be cautious without being frightened. Don't panic when a bee or wasp hovers nearby. Model calm, correct reactions so that children will know what to do to reduce their chances of getting stung in the future.

If your child has had an allergic reaction to a sting, you should talk to your pediatrician about whether a bee allergy kit would be of value.

Bleeding

Avoiding the Problem

The key to avoiding excessive bleeding in young children is supervision and prevention of injuries. Many parents remember to cover electrical outlets and put latches on drawers and cabinets, yet they forget about kitchen utensils, tools, and drinking glasses. The dishwasher is a dangerous place for infants and young children, so make sure that yours is always closed and locked. Also, keep appliances such as food processors and blenders away from the hands of small ones.

 PARENT SMART: Consider asking friends to come over to your home to sleuth for hidden dangers. Ask them to crawl around on their hands and knees, trying to see things that might attract curious little eyes and hands. Check to see whether your community has any baby proofing services. If you use this kind of service, make sure that the business owner is licensed and has good references.

What to Do if Your Baby Has Uncontrolled Bleeding

Uncontrolled bleeding requires immediate and constant attention. Stay with your child at all times.

Place a piece of clean cloth over the wound and, if you can, raise the body part that is bleeding above the level of your child's heart.

Do *not* use a tourniquet. **Apply direct and steady pressure to the wound for five minutes, pressing with the palm of your hand.** Do not remove your hand, even if you want to look at the cut to check the rate of bleeding.

If the bleeding goes through the cloth or gauze right away, do not remove the cloth. Instead, add more cloth on top of the wound and continue to apply pressure. At this point, go directly to the ER or dial 911, if you haven't already done this.

Regardless of whether the bleeding stops, there could be other injuries not in evidence and you should seek immediate medical care from your pediatrician or at an emergency room.

Some children are more prone than others to uncontrolled bleeding, and this can indicate a serious medical condition. If your child bruises easily, if he has excessive nosebleeds, or if normal cuts don't seem to clot quickly, you should see your child's physician.

As Your Child Grows

As your child grows older, he will begin to use sharp instruments such as scissors and get into new places, so you must continue to be vigilant.

When your child is ready to use scissors or a knife, you should take the time to teach him about proper use and safety precautions. Even though the tools and utensils he uses initially will be dull, he will come across similar items that are not child-safe, and he should know the proper way to carry and use them.

In rare cases, uncontrolled bleeding can be a sign of hemophilia or other illnesses. This can only be diagnosed by blood tests, and the condition may not be caught until an infant is old enough to do things that may cause excessive bleeding or easy bruising. If your child does have hemophilia, your doctor will help you and your child understand the appropriate treatments and precautions you should take.

Breathing Problems

Understanding the Problem

Babies breathe differently than older children and adults do. A newborn breathes much more rapidly, usually about forty times a minute. While babies sleep, their breathing will slow down to half their waking rate.

 PARENT SMART: Sometimes parents worry unnecessarily that their baby is breathing too rapidly. Here are some guidelines to keep in mind: A newborn up to one month old breathes about forty times a minute; an infant up to one year old breathes between twenty and forty times a minute; a child one to twelve years old normally breathes sixteen to twenty times a minute; and an adolescent breathes twelve to sixteen times a minute.

Perfectly healthy babies can also have irregular breathing patterns—they may periodically take a break of a few seconds (but fewer than ten seconds) and then pick up rapid breathing again. When babies are upset or crying, they will breathe faster than normal. For a baby who is calm, anything over sixty breaths per minute is cause for concern.

Irregular breathing, or the sudden onset of breathing difficulty, requires medical attention. These can signal heart or lung problems or may indicate a reaction to medication or something that has been ingested.

What to Do if Your Baby Is Having Trouble Breathing

Get immediate medical help if you notice any of the following:

- The baby's breathing is erratic or distressed, or with great effort.

- The baby is retracting her chest muscles—pulling in the ribcage, the area below the breastbone, or the area above the collarbones—in an effort to draw a full breath.

- The baby has bluish coloring, which can indicate respiratory and heart problems.

- The baby is flaring her nostrils repeatedly—this can be a sign that she is trying to draw in needed air.

- The baby makes unusual grunting sounds—he or she may be trying to hold or draw additional oxygen into the lungs and may be struggling to breathe. Moaning while exhaling may also indicate breathing problems.

- The baby demonstrates a pattern of frequent coughing or choking, which may indicate a breathing or digestive problem. Consult with your pediatrician immediately, or call 911, if you notice frequent or unusual coughing and choking.

As Your Child Grows

Asthma affects an estimated 10 to 12 percent of children in the United States, and, although the condition may be difficult to diagnose in infants, early identification is important. Understanding what triggers the asthma, such as dust mites, pollen, or animal dander, is the most important part of controlling it. See "Asthma" to learn more about this condition in infants and young children.

Broken Bones

Avoiding the Problem

Although the risk of broken bones increases as older children become more active and begin to run and jump and play more roughly, babies and young children do break bones in falls and other accidents. Newborns may even have bones broken (particularly collarbones) following a difficult or traumatic birth process.

A fracture is a partial or complete break of a bone. Compound fractures, also called open fractures, result in a piece of bone protruding through the skin. In a closed, or simple, fracture, the bone is broken, but the skin is intact. Incomplete fractures are more common in children, since their more-pliable bones are less likely to snap or separate completely.

The best way to prevent broken bones in babies and young children is to prevent falls from changing tables, countertops, strollers, shopping carts, and the like (see "Drops and Falls").

What to Do if Your Baby Has a Broken Bone

Symptoms may differ at various ages and from child to child. The most common symptoms of a fracture include:

- Pain and swelling in the injured area

- Visible disfiguration in the injured area

- Difficulty using or moving the injured limb

- Warmth, bruising, or redness in the injured area

If any of these symptoms appear, you should contact your child's pediatrician immediately. ER evaluation is usually indicated whenever a fracture is suspected. Always err on the side of caution in getting medical attention. A careful medical evaluation may turn up concurrent injuries.

Occasionally in breech and other difficult deliveries, an infant will have a broken clavicle. In such a case, the baby will naturally underuse the arm on the side of the broken clavicle. Bruising may be visible in the area of the broken bone. If you suspect that your baby has a broken collarbone, contact his pediatrician immediately. Immobilizing the arm and shoulder will allow rapid healing to begin. Newborns are fragile, but they are incredibly resilient and bones repair quickly and naturally.

As Your Child Grows

Recent studies indicate that almost half of American children don't get enough calcium in their diets, putting them at risk for bone weakness later in life. There are even more teens at risk for calcium deficiency. Broken bones and other health problems can be prevented or mitigated by making sure your kids get plenty of calcium as they are growing.

PARENT SMART: Make your pediatrician aware if you are adding calcium supplements, or any nonfood supplement, to your child's diet.

Burns

Avoiding the Problem

Minor burns are a common experience for babies and very young children, who will often reach for hot things out of curiosity. Burns, which include any injury to the skin caused by heat, fall into three categories:

- First-degree burns (such as sunburn) are the mildest burns. They usually cause the skin to redden but do not cause blisters to form.

- Second-degree burns cause the skin to redden and blisters to form. Second-degree burns can take two to three weeks to heal.

- Third-degree burns are the most severe. They are deep burns affecting both the skin surface and deeper tissues. Third-degree burns often have a charred or white appearance on the surface, and there is usually no sensation at the point of the burn. The skin may not be able to heal on its own and may require a skin graft.

Burns can involve any number of everyday items: for example, a cup of hot coffee left unattended, an iron that has not cooled, or a pot of boiling water that spills over. Be especially vigilant around these common dangers when you are tired, and when you are multitasking with your baby around (such as cooking, talking on the phone, and feeding baby at the same time).

What to Do if Your Baby Has a Burn

Call 911 immediately if:

- Your child is less than three months old

- The burned area is large (covers a significant portion of the body)

- The burn is on the hands, neck, eye, eyelid, face, or genitalia

- The burn is second or third degree

- The burn is from an explosion, electrical current (see "Electric Shock"), gunpowder, battery acid, or other corrosive chemicals and begins to blister

- Your child is having trouble breathing or seems confused

- You see black carbon in your child's mouth

- Your child has inhaled smoke

  BABY ALERT: If the burn is due to a fire, your infant may also be in danger from smoke inhalation. If there was an explosion, your infant may have incurred a blast injury.

Do not remove clothing *unless* the burn is from contact with corrosive chemicals. In the case of a burn from corrosive chemicals, do remove all contaminated clothing and flush the skin with warm water for ten minutes (or place the child under a warm shower for ten minutes if the exposure area is large). Be careful not to let rinse water wash chemicals to other areas of the body, particularly the eyes.

In the Case of First- and Second-Degree Burns

Immediately place the burned body part in cool water (or run cool tap water over the burn) for ten minutes. This alleviates some of the discomfort of the burn and can lessen the depth of the burn as the skin and tissues cool. You can also apply a cold compress to the burned area, which may be better tolerated than cool water, but do not apply ice directly to the skin.

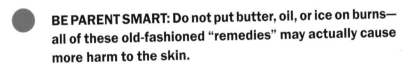 **BE PARENT SMART: Do not put butter, oil, or ice on burns— all of these old-fashioned "remedies" may actually cause more harm to the skin.**

Call your child's pediatrician immediately if you suspect that the burn is serious or bubbles into multiple blisters, blisters larger than one-half inch in width, or open blisters. Call your pediatrician if any burn becomes infected, which could happen in two to three days.

Care for minor burns at home. For first-degree burns, you can **flush the burn in cool (not ice-cold) water and then gently apply a cool compress**

over the burn to alleviate some discomfort. Keep an eye on the burn and wash very gently with mild soap and cool water once a day. Do not open closed blisters—the outer skin of the blister is the body's barrier against infection. If there are large or multiple burns, take your child to the ER.

Minor burns will probably be tender for two to three days and should peel on their own and heal within a week or so.

As Your Child Grows

Children should be taught from an early age that any fire is completely off-limits—including areas like the fireplace, stove, and barbecues. Children should never be allowed to light stoves or candles, or handle matches or lighters for any reason, and candles around the house should always be kept out of the reach of children.

Fire safety training usually begins in preschool by age three. Fire safety education should continue as the child grows. Many older children find it fun to "play" with matches and combustible substances, but this is one of the most common causes of serious fires.

Car Accidents

Avoiding the Problem

It is easy to become complacent behind the wheel. We quickly forget that driving—something most of us do routinely—is the most dangerous activity that we do each day. A crying baby (or a laughing baby, for that matter) can be a major distraction while you are navigating traffic. In addition to keeping an eye on your baby, you'll encounter other distractions, such as radio switching, cell phones, and the normal perils on the road. When children are in the car, the rules of driving should never be ignored: do not drive when overly tired, or when your concentration is impaired for any other reason; do not drive aggressively; while driving, do not talk on the cell phone, eat your lunch, or do any task that will take your attention from the road.

Attaching car-seat mirrors allows you to keep an eye on your child with a quick glance when you come to a stoplight. If you suspect that something is amiss with the car seat or you're otherwise concerned about the comfort of your baby, pull over at the next safe spot and investigate the trouble. Never reach back while driving to care for your baby.

The most important preventative measure any parent driver can make is to ensure that the car seat is properly installed and that the baby is properly secured within it. This is true even if you are just driving around the corner or moving the car to a new parking spot. Anytime the baby is in the car, he or she should be buckled in safely. There are no exceptions.

As babies get older, do not show them how to unfasten the safety harness or seatbelt on their own. Always unfasten the belt yourself. If you notice that the baby has managed to undo the buckle while you're driving, pull over at the next safe spot and refasten the buckle, adjusting the safety harness if necessary. (If this becomes a habit, you may need to install a new buckle that your baby cannot unfasten.)

In general, try to keep in-the-car chaos to a minimum. Older children and other adults should do everything they can to keep from disturbing the driver. In addition, do not keep weighty or large objects loose in the car, since they can be thrown in a collision and injure people in the car. Keep potentially dangerous objects in the trunk.

What to Do if You and Your Baby Are in a Car Accident

First, stay calm. **Turn off the ignition** to prevent a fire hazard (there may be a gasoline leak as a result of the collision). Call 911 or have a bystander call 911.

If you believe that the impact of an accident is significant, or if you are concerned that your child may have been injured (he is short of breath or he may have a neck injury, for example), **do not move your child until emergency personnel arrive on the scene**. Only if absolutely necessary—if the car is in a precarious position (near an embankment, for instance) or is in danger of catching fire—should you move your baby from the car while you wait for emergency help. Moving the child can increase the severity of the injury by causing damage to the spinal cord.

If the baby has stopped breathing, lift his chin to open the airway. If the baby does not resume breathing, remove him carefully from the car seat. Gently place the baby on his back, keeping movement to a minimum, and lift the chin again. If no response, follow procedure on fold-out CPR guide.

BABY ALERT: Have you taken an infant CPR course since the birth of your child? If not, you should contact your local hospital or American Heart Association or Red Cross chapter and enroll in a class. If you have a busy schedule, as most of us do, you can even host a CPR "home party" for you and other new parents, for a small fee. Although nothing can replace live training, there are also video programs of infant CPR, such as *Infant & Child CPR*, by Kathy Kalemba, available through many online retailers.

If the baby has been cut in the accident, apply direct pressure to the wound with tissue, clothing, or gauze, if it's available. Continue to apply pressure until help arrives. Be gentle when applying pressure to a laceration on the front of the head, in case there is also a neck injury.

If you suspect that your child has broken a bone, keep the child as immobile as possible and wait for help to arrive.

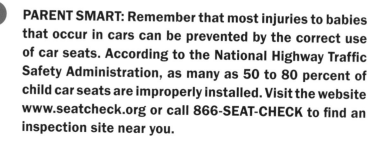

PARENT SMART: Remember that most injuries to babies that occur in cars can be prevented by the correct use of car seats. According to the National Highway Traffic Safety Administration, as many as 50 to 80 percent of child car seats are improperly installed. Visit the website www.seatcheck.org or call 866-SEAT-CHECK to find an inspection site near you.

As Your Child Grows

Your baby may seem so small and fragile, but this is not the period of his life when he is most likely to suffer injury in a car. That period will come when he is a teen. But do not wait for your child to turn sixteen before you start teaching him about safe driving. Begin right now. Studies show that the best predictor of whether teens become safe drivers is whether or not their parents are safe and careful drivers. In other words, your children are learning their driving habits from you, so make sure that you are teaching them through your actions and not just your words.

Safety Alert:
Car Injury Prevention

- A child must never be left unattended in a car seat.

- Use the car seat properly every single time you get in the car—even for the shortest trips. Never hold an infant in your lap or in a carrying harness while in the car. Babies (and, for that matter, older children and adults) should be buckled in safely whenever they are in the car.

- Once you buckle your baby into the seat, the straps should be snug everywhere. (You should be able to slide one finger under the straps.)

- The harness clip (if your car seat has one) should be set level with the baby's armpits (to keep the shoulder straps correctly placed).

- The straps should be flat and untwisted.

- Make sure the seat is clear of blankets, toys, pacifiers, and the like before you strap him or her in. Never boost a child up within the seat using books, blankets, or anything else. If your child is "slouching" to the side, you can use rolled up blankets or towels on the sides to keep him or her upright in the seat.

- The baby should be reclined comfortably at a forty-five-degree angle—make sure the baby's head cannot fall forward.

- Your car's seatbelts should be fitted with locking clips if they move when buckled. If your car seat does not have locking clips, contact the manufacturer of the car seat.

- Side air bags present a potential risk of serious injury to children—be sure to read the owner's manual for your car carefully.

- Always wear a seatbelt in the car—this keeps you and your passengers safe, and it sets a good example for children of all ages.

- Do not multitask while driving, and avoid the use of the cell phone.

Chemical Burns

Avoiding the Problem

There are many items in your home that can cause a chemical burn, including bleach, drain or toilet-bowl cleaner, metal cleaners, and pool chlorinators. All toxic products should be kept in locked cabinets far out of the reach of children.

 BABY ALERT: Fumes from toxic cleaners can also be harmful to your infant. Never use toxic products when your infant is in the room.

When you need to use these products, try to use them when your child is asleep or being cared for by another responsible adult in another room. It only takes a second for curious hands to tip over a bottle or open a lid, and any contact with the skin and in particular the eyes will be dangerous. Also make sure that you wear protective gloves and clothing when you handle these products. Respecting dangerous substances should be a habit, and one that you should pass on to your children.

What to Do if Your Child Has a Chemical Burn

Chemical burns require emergency medical attention. Immediately call 911, or the American Association of Poison Control Centers at 800-222-1222. You can also call your local poison control center. You will need to manage the burn until help arrives or until you are given further directions over the phone.

 BABY ALERT: If possible, read the label of the substance that has caused the chemical burn right away. The label may give you important information regarding what you should or should not do.

When a child comes in contact with a chemical substance, in most cases you should **wash the area with water for twenty minutes**.

If the chemical has gotten into your child's eye, **rinse the eye with water continuously**, preferably in the shower. Your child will not like having his eye held open and irrigated, or washed, but this can be an important and necessary step. When irrigating the eye, be careful not to contaminate the other eye.

Do not touch the area affected by the burn, but **cover the area with a clean, dry cloth after rinsing**. Do not apply any ointments or creams on the burned area without first consulting a physician. Take your child to your pediatrician or to the emergency room immediately.

As Your Child Grows

Even when your child is older, you should always keep toxic and hazardous products in a locked cabinet. When your child observes you using potentially dangerous products, give her detailed explanations of the dangers and also emphasize that they should never be taken out or played with.

Children should never be asked to help out with household chores when toxic or dangerous products are involved. Even though some children are careful and highly responsible, they do not have the motor coordination, reaction speed, or strength of an adult and are much more likely to unintentionally cause an accident than adults. By thirteen or fourteen most children are able to handle chores that might involve toxic materials, but even at this age careful safety instruction should be given. Teens with impulse control or attention problems should continue to be closely supervised.

C

Choking

Avoiding the Problem

Babies and young children investigate their world relentlessly, and a favorite way to find out about interesting objects is to put them in their mouths. Any object that is small enough to obstruct the baby's airway may result in a choking emergency. Most choking accidents can be prevented by following a few prevention tips. Balloons, coins, buttons, nuts, popcorn—anything babies can put in their mouths—should be kept away from your baby.

Mild coughing when your child first begins to eat solid food is normal. Here are a few tips for feeding your baby safely:

- Even after your baby begins eating solid foods, and up to about age four, be careful not to give him any foods that are hard or difficult to swallow, such as popcorn, raw carrots, or grapes. Hot dogs are a very common cause of choking problems.

- All food should be cut into very small or very thin pieces to prevent choking.

- Do not give young children things like peanuts that are hard and smooth and require advanced chewing.

- Your child should always be seated when eating—don't allow babies or young children to eat while crawling, walking, or playing.

- Don't let older children feed the baby unsupervised.

Toys present a particular danger for babies. Select toys that match the age guidelines for your child. Toys meant for older children may have small parts that present a choking danger and should be kept out of the reach of your baby. Children under three should not have any toys smaller than an inch in diameter and two inches in length. Before settling your child in any play area, check carefully (including behind cushions and under furniture) for any objects that present a choking hazard. Do the same thing when you are visiting a relative's home or friend's home.

PARENT SMART: Did you know that 90 percent of deaths of children under five are caused by choking? Of these deaths, 65 percent occur in infants. There are services in most communities that will "baby proof" your home by covering electrical outlets and securing drawers and doors, but keeping small objects away from your baby is an ongoing chore that you must do constantly.

What to Do if Your Baby Starts Choking

If an infant is coughing hard and crying, this is likely due to a partial obstruction and your baby may clear the obstruction himself without your doing anything. **However, you will need to intervene if:**

- He is unable to breathe

- He is having trouble coughing

- He cannot make the usual sounds or verbalizations

- He has a very red or blue facial color or blue lips

> **BABY ALERT: Your baby's organs are fragile—do not attempt to perform the Heimlich maneuver as you would on an adult or older child. See the instructions in the back of this book for the correct way to dislodge something caught in a baby's air passage.**

First, if someone is in the room with you, have that person **call 911**, or call 911 yourself. If you see something in your child's mouth that you can easily remove, do so.

Place the infant (twelve months or younger) facedown on your forearm in a head-down position with the head and neck stabilized. Rest

your forearm firmly against your body for additional support. **For a larger baby, you may lay the baby facedown across your lap, with his head lower than the rest of his body. Give five rapid blows between the baby's shoulder blades with the heel of your hand.** (See the fold-out diagram at the back of this book.)

If the baby is still not breathing, **gently turn the baby onto his back on a firm surface and, using two fingers, deliver five rapid chest compressions on the lower half of the breastbone** (one finger's breadth below the nipples).

If the baby is unconscious, you must take immediate action to open the airway. Place the palm of your hand on the baby's forehead and tilt the head back. With your other hand, lift the baby's chin forward. Do not try to remove the obstructing object unless you can see it. If you can see it, sweep it out of the airway with your finger. **Repeat back blows and chest thrusts.**

C

● BABY ALERT: See the Heimlich maneuver instructions and the fold-out diagram of what to do when your baby is choking and how to perform baby CPR in the back of this book. **Please note: there are different procedures for infants (under one year) and older babies (over one year).** We urge all parents to take a baby CPR class from your local hospital, the American Red Cross, or the American Heart Association. There is no substitute for this kind of training, and it may save your baby's life. Do not consider yourself adequately trained to deal with choking until you have completed this course.

As Your Child Grows

Even older children can be susceptible to choking accidents. An estimated seventy-three hundred children choke on things like hard candies, hot dogs, and small objects each year. Make sure that all adults who care for your children—babysitters, teachers, even grandparents—have annual classes on CPR along with a review of general first aid.

Crying (Inconsolable)

Understanding the Problem

Babies cry as a way to communicate. Their cries may mean "I'm hungry," "I'm full," "I'm tired," "I need a diaper change," "I'm irritated," "I'm frustrated," "I'm afraid," or "I'm bored." Of course, the most important cry is the one that says "I'm in pain."

Babies cry in almost the same way whether they are experiencing external or internal pain. This cry begins without warning, and it is loud, long, and shrill. Your baby will let out a long wail of pain, and then she will take a long pause, like she is holding her breath. When she cries again, her body language will also tell you that something is really wrong. Her body will be tense, and her hands and feet will be drawn up. Her mouth will be wide open and you will see an expression of intense discomfort on her face.

If your baby goes through many periods of inconsolable crying and is between three weeks and three months old, he may have colic. Colic occurs in an estimated 20 to 25 percent of infants and is best defined using the "rule of three":

- The infant cries for more than three hours a day, usually at night.

- The infant has a period of excessive crying at least three days a week.

- This pattern continues for at least three consecutive weeks in an otherwise healthy baby.

Crying due to colic typically has a rapid and abrupt onset with little buildup. More disturbing to parents, the baby does not seem to be able to stop crying—the crying just continues without any sense of ebb or flow. In addition, there are also distinct physical signs that a baby exhibits during these periods of intense crying. The stomach will tighten, fists will clench, and legs and knees will be drawn up. Many infants look like they are holding their breath during these periods of crying. Babies' faces become red, their feet become cold, and they may become pale around the mouth.

What to Do if Your Baby Is Crying Inconsolably

For a Cry of Pain

The first thing you need to do is to **check for external causes of pain**. Is a toe or finger caught in a zipper? Does the baby have a rash? Is any clothing too tight? Is hair causing a tourniquet around fingers, toes, or penis? Often you will have to take off all your child's clothes to check that everything is all right.

A cry of internal pain, of course, is more difficult to determine, since it may be caused by an ear infection, a sore throat, a stomachache, or a scratched cornea.

If this type of crying continues, you will certainly want to call your pediatrician, and you should describe what you see as well as what you hear. The physical signs that accompany a baby's pain may include redness; swelling; sensitivity to touch; a fever; a change in bowel movements (including a change in color or smell); vomiting; and noisy, fast, or difficult breathing. You should also tell your doctor about a change in mood and behavior. Does your baby bat at or touch her ears? Has she been eating and sleeping normally? Has she been more fretful than usual?

For Colic

If your baby has been diagnosed with colic, you will want to try a number of things that have been known to console babies with colic, including rhythmic rocking, swaddling, giving your child a warm bath, singing, taking your child for a ride in the car, turning on rhythmic noises (like a washing machine), or giving your baby a massage. Every baby is different, and some of these ideas may comfort your baby while others will not. Your baby will certainly let you know what works and what doesn't.

Above all, remember that colic is a stage that rarely lasts past three or four months of age. If your baby has colic, don't blame yourself. **Get help with taking care of your baby so that you can get enough sleep. If you don't get sleep, you will have a more difficult time coping, your baby's crying will seem that much worse, and you will be less able to help your child.**

As Your Child Grows

Your baby has many different types of cries, and researchers tell us that most parents become expert at distinguishing one cry from another. Most babies significantly decrease their crying between four and six months of age, both due to the babies' development as well as to the parents' growing awareness of what to do to stop the crying.

There may be times, however, when your baby will cry again. Separation from you may cause your baby to cry inconsolably as early as six to nine months, but the real tears and wails of separation usually come between twelve and eighteen months. Do be sympathetic, reassuring, and loving when you must leave your child in the capable hands of a caregiver or family member, but keep in mind that giving in at this age does not help and may prolong the baby's crying. Your baby needs to learn how to calm himself down when he is upset, and he won't be able to do this if you don't let him experience normal stress. If you believe that your toddler or preschooler is much more anxious than other children of the same age, then you should seek advice from a qualified professional. Anxiety disorders are one of the most common psychological problems experienced by children and teens, and many of these can be prevented through early intervention.

Cuts

Avoiding the Problem

Cuts and scrapes are a fact of life for all children. Be as vigilant as possible about sharp edges around the house and in public places, especially playgrounds. Obviously, scissors, knives, and other sharp-edged objects should be kept well out of reach and locked away from children.

What to Do if Your Baby Is Cut

With minor cuts and scrapes, **first make sure that the wound is clean**—remove any glass, dirt, or other debris by flushing the cut in cool, running water. If necessary, use tweezers to remove splinters or other foreign material. Once it's clean, if the wound is bleeding, **apply direct pressure to the cut with a clean towel or bandage**. Once the bleeding has stopped, clean the wound very gently with soap and water and rinse for five minutes or so.

If the cut or scrape is small, and if your child is not likely to pick at the cut, leave it uncovered—it will heal faster in the open air. You may apply over-the-counter antibiotic ointment if your child does not have allergies to it and isn't likely to rub it off or get it into her mouth.

If you need to use a bandage, make sure the skin is clean and dry. Once the cut scabs over, you can get rid of the bandage (unless you want to protect the cut from scratching). If the cut becomes infected in the next two to three days, call your pediatrician.

If the cut is deep or won't stop bleeding, apply even pressure with a clean cloth or paper towel (or a bandage, if available). If the bleeding has not slowed or stopped after about five to seven minutes or looks as if it needs stitches, **head to the emergency room**. It's always a good idea to check with your doctor about cuts to the face, since these can leave scars and may benefit from additional treatment. If a cut was caused by something unclean (such as rusty playground equipment), your physician may also recommend a tetanus booster.

> BABY ALERT: If you are not sure how the cut occurred, it is best to visit your pediatrician or go directly to the ER to make sure that there are no foreign bodies retained in the wound. This is particularly important if your child steps on something.

In the case of a puncture wound (for instance, if a child steps on a rusty nail), **wash the area with soap and water**. Apply antibiotic ointment to the area and cover the wound with a bandage. Minor puncture wounds generally bleed less than cuts do, but still carry the risk of a foreign body imbedded in the skin, so you should go to the emergency room. In any case, contact your physician immediately—he or she may prescribe medicine to prevent infection or may recommend a tetanus booster. (If you have been visiting the pediatrician regularly, your baby's tetanus shots are probably up to date—but you should still check with the pediatrician to make sure this is the case.)

 BABY ALERT: Generally speaking, cuts that are more than one-quarter inch deep, have jagged edges, or edges that gape open will need stitches. Lacerations over any joint should be evaluated in an emergency room. Wounds that require sutures should be evaluated as soon as possible. Waiting increases the risk of infection and/or scarring.

As Your Child Grows

As older children begin expanding their outdoor activities, make sure they steer clear of potential danger areas like the garage, tool shed, and construction sites—anywhere sharp objects, chemicals, and other hazards abound. Teach children never to handle knives or scissors; tell them that if they find something sharp around the house or outside they should let you know about it rather than trying to move it themselves.

Diaper Rashes

Avoiding the Problem

Diaper rash is a common trouble that usually causes no more than mild irritation where the diaper comes in contact with the baby's skin. In some cases, however, the rash may worsen into blisters, pimples, and sores that may become infected. An infected rash will develop more intense discoloration of the skin and may be swollen. The rash may spread beyond the immediate diaper area, appearing in the form of patches of reddish, irritated skin elsewhere on the body.

Most cases of diaper rash can be prevented by keeping your baby's bottom clean, dry, and cool. Change diapers often and let your baby go diaper-free whenever possible—a nap on an open cloth diaper (with a plastic or waterproof sheet protecting the mattress) can offer a nice break from diapers and diaper changes.

Cloth and disposable diapers each have their advantages. Some suggest that disposable diapers absorb more liquid (thereby preventing diaper rash), while others advocate using all-cotton cloth diapers, since you're likely to change them more often and thereby prevent diaper rash. If you use cloth diapers, after you wash them it is recommended that you boil them for fifteen minutes on the stove to kill germs and to get rid of residual soap that may irritate your baby's skin.

Diapers that are fastened too snugly or left on too long can cause irritation, as can plastic or rubber pants that fit over diapers. Avoid using them or anything else that increases heat and moisture in the diaper area, as both exacerbate rashes and can cause irritation to the skin. Ointments that contain zinc oxide (such as Desitin) help to keep the diaper area dry and help to prevent rashes. However, avoid using talcum powder (which can be inhaled by babies) and cornstarch (which can exacerbate infections caused by yeast). Diaper rash may appear or worsen when a baby has diarrhea.

What to Do if Your Baby Has Diaper Rash

You should **call your pediatrician if any diaper rash appears during the baby's first six weeks.**

Beyond six weeks, you should contact your pediatrician if:

- The rash persists for more than a week

- The rash becomes infected

- The rash develops blisters or ulcers

- The baby has lost his or her appetite

- Bumps, hives, or nodules appear

- Bleeding begins

- The rash spreads to other parts of the body

- The baby has a fever

When a baby has mild diaper rash, small changes in diaper hygiene should take care of it—rinse the area with warm water between diapers and make sure the diaper area is completely dry before putting on a new diaper. Some babies are sensitive to the chemicals in a particular brand of diapers, soap, or baby wipes. If a rash develops and persists, try changing brands to see if the trouble clears up. Consult with your pediatrician about the best way to handle mild diaper rashes at home.

Some rashes are simply irritations, but most rashes are caused by bacteria and yeast. Yeast, which is a part of the natural flora of our skin, can infect rashes that are left untreated. Heat and moisture also encourage yeast infections. If your baby has frequent yeast infections, make an appointment to see your pediatrician, since there may be other health concerns to address.

As Your Child Grows

Most toddlers are ready to stop using diapers between two and three years of age. The good news is that you will no longer have the expense of diapers, the worry about changing diapers, and the inevitable rashes. The bad news is that, for some children, toilet training can be a prolonged and exhausting process. Be patient. This too shall pass.

Diarrhea

Avoiding the Problem

Diarrhea is a common problem that tends to appear as your infant's digestive tract accommodates changes in diet and his environment. It is not particularly pleasant, but it is usually not serious. However, chronic diarrhea, which persists for four weeks or more, can both be an indicator of a serious underlying medical problem and can cause additional serious health problems through severe dehydration.

Severe diarrhea is most often caused by viruses, sometimes by bacteria or parasites, but it can also suggest other pathology. In the very young, severe dehydration can happen very quickly. In addition to experiencing worsening diarrhea, babies may have abdominal pain after a bowel movement in the case of severe diarrhea. Infections may also cause fever, low appetite, and vomiting. Diarrhea usually subsides on its own within a few days, but it can last longer if underlying conditions are not addressed. Chronic diarrhea can keep infants from thriving (failing to grow at normal, healthy rates) or it may cause them to lose weight. Blood in a baby's stool can be an indication of a more serious condition requiring an immediate call to your pediatrician.

In the United States, diarrhea is most often caused by food that has been handled or processed improperly, by contaminated water, or by contagions passed between people (common in day-care centers). The best protection against contagious viruses and bacteria that cause diarrhea is frequent hand washing. Wash your baby's hands after he's been outside, and always before he eats. Wash fruits and vegetables carefully before feeding them to your baby.

What to Do if Your Baby Has Severe or Chronic Diarrhea

If your child has severe diarrhea, sustained diarrhea, bloody diarrhea, or diarrhea in combination with vomiting, fever, or abdominal pain, call your pediatrician to make an appointment. **Call your pediatrician immediately if your baby seems dehydrated—symptoms can include pallor, dry lips and tongue, sunken eyes, lethargy, and diminished urination** (in infants, fewer than six wet diapers a day can be a sign of dehydration). **If you suspect serious dehydration and cannot contact your pediatrician, head to the emergency room.**

As Your Child Grows

Teach children good hand-washing habits. Frequent, thorough soaping and rinsing are the best defense against viral and bacterial infections.

Drops and Falls

Avoiding the Problem

By the age of four or five months, your baby will develop enough muscle control to wriggle, grab, and roll over. She may crawl by six to eight months and take her first step as early as ten months. In all of these stages of exploration, babies are at risk for spills and falls. They are also vulnerable to accidental drops from beds, changing tables, and even the arms of caregivers.

Most falls are not emergencies, and almost all falls can be prevented by vigilance on the part of caregivers. However, it is important to remember that even if a fall is not from a dangerous height, babies are always at risk for landing on sharp table corners or harmful objects, or suffering head injuries.

Here are some tips for preventing falls:

- Never leave an infant unattended on a changing table or bed. If you need to step away to answer the phone, to grab a diaper, or to attend to anything else, take the baby with you.

- Try to use changing tables with guardrails at least two inches high. Make use of the safety belt on changing tables in public places—as well as in strollers and high chairs.

- Always secure your baby with safety belts and harnesses when they are available. Anytime you put a belt or harness on a child, be certain you know how to use it correctly and that there is no possibility of strangulation.

- Children should never play on fire escapes, balconies, high porches, and the like.

- Do not use a walker for your baby. According to the American Academy of Pediatrics, fourteen thousand children end up in the hospital each year from falls or other accidents involving baby walkers. A baby in a walker is at risk of tumbling over hard objects in her path, knocking into a hot stove, or even rolling down stairs or into a backyard swimming pool.

- Do not rely on window screens to prevent children from falling from windows. If you open windows, try to do so by sliding down the top half of the window, or use window guards (required by law in some cities). If you must open windows from the bottom, do not open them more than four inches.

- Children can squeeze through as little as five inches of space, so even if a window looks only slightly open it may still be a hazard to children. Don't keep chairs, stools, or other furniture near windowsills.

- Stairs can be a major hazard, even when all the best precautions, such as security gates, have been taken. Never leave a child unsupervised around stairs—even gated stairs. Babies (from a surprisingly early age) may be able to climb over the gate and can fall down stairs. Avoid accordion gates—these can pinch children, and babies and young children might be able to fit their heads through them and become injured.

- Never place your baby in a car safety seat, infant seat, or other carrier atop tabletops or other furniture. The baby's movements within the seat may cause the seat to topple off a countertop or tabletop, causing serious injury.

- Between seven and ten months, babies begin to hoist themselves up by holding on to furniture (or anything else in reach). Be sure that all top-heavy or unwieldy furniture (such as bookcases or entertainment centers) are secured to the wall with L-brackets to keep them from tipping away from the wall.

- Wrap corners of coffee tables, countertops, and other furniture with sharp edges in protective padding. These pads can be purchased ready made (designed to fit table corners), or you can fashion your own; regardless of what padding you use, make sure it's substantial and securely in place.

- Always keep the rails up on the side of the crib. Once your baby starts standing in the crib, remove bumpers so that she can't use them to climb over the crib railing.

PARENT SMART: Always be sure that your crib meets current safety standards. Old cribs inherited from friends or relatives may look sturdy, but they may have hidden dangers.

What to Do if Your Baby Falls

If your baby has been seriously injured in a fall, call for immediate medical attention. If you are concerned that bones may have been broken, keep the baby as immobile as possible. If there is the possibility of a neck injury, do not move the baby unless not doing so causes further danger (e.g., in the case of a fire). If you must move the baby, be careful not to let the neck move.

If the fall was from furniture (or other height) or involved a blow to the head, call your pediatrician, even if the baby seems all right after the accident. Children under two months of age may require further testing. If your child is bleeding, please see "Cuts."

 BABY ALERT: You should visit an emergency room any time your child under two years of age has what you consider a significant fall and you are unable to speak to your child's pediatrician.

As Your Child Grows

Give children the training they need to operate safely in the world as soon as they are ready. Your child has only observed adults going down the stairs forward—once your child is about a year old, show her how to go down the stairs backward, or by sitting on the stairs and moving down one stair at a time.

As children get older, they are still prone to falls as they charge through the world with seemingly boundless energy. In fact, most serious falls occur when children are older, particularly on the playground (more than a quarter of a million children under fourteen go to the hospital each year as a result of playground falls). Keep kids of all ages away from trampolines (even if you are watching them). Inspect playgrounds for unsafe equipment that is broken, sharp, wobbly, or rusty. Playgrounds should also be founded on soft, absorbent material to reduce the shock of falls. Steer clear of playgrounds built on concrete or hard dirt surfaces.

Drowning

Avoiding the Problem

Babies and young children are drawn to water out of curiosity and a desire to play. But water is also a deadly danger for babies. A baby can drown in as little as two inches of water. Any container that holds water—a tub, a wading pool, even a toilet—is of concern.

If you have a swimming pool, a four-sided fence around the pool is an absolute necessity (and usually a legal requirement). Make sure any neighbors with backyard pools also have fencing that blocks all access to the swimming pool. Fencing should be *at least* 4 feet high (some municipalities require taller fences, so check your local regulations to make sure you're in compliance). There should be no spaces between bars or other parts of the fence through which a baby or child could squeeze (no gaps larger than 4 inches). The gate should be self-latching and self-closing, and it should open away from the pool, so babies and children can't use their weight to push the gate open. (Have the fence and gate in place before your child can crawl or walk—that day is bound to catch you by surprise, and it's better to be prepared well in advance of a baby's first explorations.) If you have a pool, it's also important to have safety equipment close by (life preservers approved by the U.S. Coast Guard, shepherd's hook, and other equipment). Don't rely on floaties, water wings, or other recreational flotation devices in the case of an emergency!

D

Always be sure to support the baby's head throughout his bath and never leave an infant unattended in the bath—no matter how carefully settled he is into a bathing ring or other contraption. Babies can easily tip and fall from such devices and can drown in as little as an inch or two of water. Even if the tub is empty, babies and young children should never be left alone in the bathroom—toilets also present a drowning hazard. Never leave water standing in buckets, sinks, baby pools, or other containers.

Be sure that all caregivers understand that infants should never be left unattended or under the supervision of another child near any body of water—including bathtubs, pools, ponds, or irrigation ditches. Infant bath seats and other flotation devices

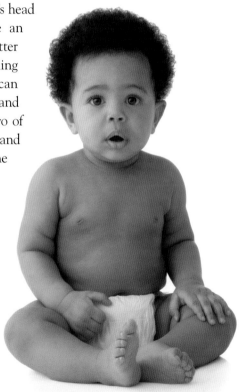

for swimming and bathing cannot protect an unsupervised child and are no substitute for grown-up supervision (even for a moment).

Child safety experts suggest that an adult supervisor should be within arm's length of all babies and young children the entire time they are near swimming pools or other bodies of water.

What to Do if Your Baby Has a Drowning Accident

Even with the greatest possible vigilance and all precautions being taken, accidents happen. Knowing what to do the moment you see an infant or child drowning might mean the difference between life and death. **If your infant or child is drowning or is unconscious in the water:**

1. Get the child out of the water and lay him on a flat surface. There may be a concurrent neck injury, especially if the child has landed on his face or head when diving into the water. Try not to move the child's neck, but support the head gently.

2. Check for breathing and if not breathing, give 2 rescue breaths and **SEE THE FOLD-OUT CPR GUIDE FOR WHAT TO DO NEXT.**

3. Once the child begins breathing, cover him with towels and blankets and call 911 if this has not been done already.

As Your Child Grows

Teach all children to swim.

Some people begin teaching children as young as six months how to kick in the pool, though most children are not ready for formal swimming lessons until about their fourth birthday. There are always opportunities to teach children good water safety—by instruction and by example. Even if your child learns to swim early, you must continue to provide close supervision in and around the pool and other bodies of water.

At the beginning of every summer, review water safety rules with your children and teenagers.

Eating Problems

Avoiding the Problem

Almost all babies go through periods of fussiness around mealtime (and some babies, of course, are temperamentally inclined to be fussy). These problems can be lessened, to a certain extent, by making dietary changes gradually and introducing new foods one at a time, starting with the easiest foods to digest. A baby who has been difficult at mealtime for a stretch of weeks or months might be having digestive problems that make mealtime unpleasant for her (and certainly for you). Persistent eating problems can be a sign of colic, food allergies, reflux, and other digestive problems.

What to Do if Your Baby Has Eating Problems

Loss of appetite can be a sign of illness. In combination with persistent vomiting and an abdomen that is distended or tender, eating problems can be a sign of a serious condition such as severe infection or intestinal blockage. **If your baby shows persistent vomiting, has bloody stool, or has a distended or tender abdomen, seek immediate medical attention.**

Keep in mind that underfeeding can be harmful. Make an appointment to see your physician if your baby shows diminished appetite, is listless, or loses weight.

As Your Child Grows

Obesity has become a serious health problem in the United States, and obesity in children is at its highest historic rate. Healthy eating habits should be set early on and maintained through childhood. Eating healthfully (a diet low in fats and sugars, and high in vegetables and whole grains) and eating together at regular mealtimes will help to establish good habits for a lifetime. Avoid letting kids eat candy as a regular snack between meals, and don't let them eat in front of the television set. Having consistent, healthy, and happy eating experiences in childhood makes eating healthfully in adulthood second nature.

 PARENT SMART: Many people have their own ideas about special diets for children. Some may be based on sound nutrition, but others are not. Children do require some fat and other essential nutrients in their diet, for proper brain, nervous system, and muscle development. Always consult your physician before putting your child on any kind of diet.

Electric Shock

Avoiding the Problem

Survey your home for electrical hazards, including outlets and extension cords. Outlet covers are available at local hardware and baby stores. Most communities have services that will "baby proof" your home, making it much safer for infants and toddlers. However, don't be misled into thinking that any environment is 100-percent safe. Accidents happen even when you take every imaginable precaution, and keeping a home safe is a daily chore.

> **BABY ALERT: Always make sure that there are no electrical appliances such as radios or hair dryers nearby that might fall or be pulled into a bathtub. Although babies will instinctively pull away if they come in contact with a current and usually do so in time to prevent a shock, any shock to the mouth or wet hands (or while the baby is standing in water) can cause serious and potentially life-threatening injury.**

Appliance and lamp cords as well as extension cords are a serious danger, particularly if they are old or frayed. Some babies put extension cords in their mouths, and teething babies may chew on the cords. Unplug and remove extension cords when they are not in use. Take care to check extension cords before you use them and replace any that have cracked, worn, or otherwise damaged surfaces.

What to Do if Your Baby Experiences Electric Shock

In the event of an electric shock, your first instinct will be to yank a child away from the source of the current. DON'T DO THIS. When you touch the child, any coursing electrical currents will extend to you and make you unable to help your child.

First, switch off the source of the current. Unplug the appliance or lamp. If it is not possible to turn off the electricity, separate the child from the current using something dry and nonconductive—such as a wooden broomstick. Pull your child far enough away from the source that the current cannot reconnect.

Once the child is safely away from the current, **check his breathing and pulse.** Put your ear close to your child's nose to **listen for breath while you watch for the rise and fall of the chest. If the child is not breathing, give 2 breaths and follow the CPR procedure on the fold-out guide.** (Remember to sign up for your CPR class if you haven't already done so.)

If the child is breathing (or resumes breathing), **check immediately for burns. Apply cool, wet cloths to first- and second-degree burns** (see "Burns"). Keep affected areas elevated while you wait for emergency medical help to arrive. **Do not touch third-degree burns** (skin may look charred, black, or white).

> **BABY ALERT:** Even if he seems to have suffered only mild burns from an electric shock, call 911 or head immediately to the emergency room. Electric shock may damage internal organs, and the body may go into shock minutes or hours after a traumatic injury. Signs of shock include restlessness, anxiety, nausea, vomiting, and pale, cold, or clammy skin. If you suspect the onset of shock after a traumatic injury, elevate the child's feet and cover him with a blanket until emergency medical help arrives or until you arrive at the emergency room.

As Your Child Grows

Toddlers and even older children need to be reminded that electricity and electrical appliances are dangerous and should never be played with or treated lightly. Teach children never to play with outlets, cords, or wires.

Also, don't forget to teach your children about lightning and what to do in a storm. Shelter should be sought when a thunderstorm is approaching—not after it has struck. During a thunderstorm, children and adults should stay away from trees, flagpoles, and other tall structures, as well as open fields (where they may the tallest object in the area). It's important, of course, to get out of a swimming pool or any body of water when a storm is approaching.

Failure to Bond

Understanding the Problem

Occasionally babies do not seem to bond with their parents. They may not make eye contact, they may not respond to their name, they may not seem to smile like other babies do, and they may not like to be cuddled or even touched.

This kind of behavior can be an early warning sign of a developmental problem, and professional advice should be sought as soon as possible. This behavior can be a sign of an emotional or neurological disorder, such as autism spectrum disorder, but it can also be an indication of other problems. Early detection and intervention are essential.

Here are five symptoms common to children who are later diagnosed with a disorder on the autistic spectrum:

1. By three months, the infant does not consistently respond to his name and may respond selectively to sounds of the same volume.

2. By the first year, the infant does not participate in "joint attention." He may not follow another person's gaze, look at where another person points, or even show an object or toy to a parent.

3. By ten months, the child does not imitate the facial expressions or gestures of others.

4. By ten months, the child does not respond reciprocally to the emotions of others, such as smiling when a person smiles at her, crying when another baby is crying, or showing curiosity at the sight of older children.

5. By eighteen to twenty-four months, the child does not seem interested in pretend play, such as with dolls or trucks, and may not seem interested in toys at all.

What to Do if Your Baby Does Not Bond with You

If a child does not meet the developmental milestones listed here, **contact your child's pediatrician**. A complete developmental evaluation should be performed. This kind of testing is available by contacting your state education office, which will find a team of experts to assess your baby. You should be aware that funding is available both to assess and treat infants and children with developmental disabilities.

As Your Child Grows

There are many children born with emotional or neurological problems that inhibit their bonding. The good news is that there is a great deal of interest in these problems, and we are constantly learning new treatment techniques. Whatever the cause of the problem, early intervention will result in a much better prognosis.

Fever

Avoiding the Problem

Fevers are an inevitable part of childhood, and the majority of fevers should not be any cause for concern (with the important exception of fevers in children under two or three months old).

Fevers develop when the hypothalamus (the part of the brain that regulates body temperature) resets the body to a higher temperature, usually in response to infection or illness.

Fevers can also be caused by overdressing infants—so make sure your baby is dressed in light, breathable clothes unless cold temperatures require bundling up. Vaccines, exertion, teething, and normal temperature fluctuations during the day may raise a baby's body temperature slightly, but this is not usually a cause for concern.

If a fever is prolonged or dangerously high, however, dehydration and other potential health emergencies can develop.

You can often tell if your child has a fever simply by feeling his forehead. Doctors recommend using a digital thermometer in order to get the most accurate temperature reading. In infants and very young children, doctors recommend taking temperature rectally with a digital thermometer. In children over four, taking the temperature orally or under the arm can be helpful, as can using an ear thermometer (the ear canals of infants are usually too small to use an ear thermometer effectively).

What to Do if Your Child Has a High Fever

Seek emergency medical attention if a feverish baby has any of the following:

- Extreme irritability or inconsolable crying that lasts for hours

- Lethargy, muscle weakness, or paralysis

- Rash or purple splotches that resemble bruises (and appear after the onset of the fever)

- Blue lips, tongue, and nails

- Protruding fontanelle (the soft spot on a baby's head)

- Stiff neck or headache

- Difficulty breathing

- Seizure

- Rectal temperature of 100.4° or greater

If your child has a fever but is otherwise eating well, playing, and happy, it's best to let the fever run its natural course. Make sure the baby is well hydrated and getting plenty of fluids, be careful not to overdress him, and make sure he gets plenty of rest. If fever symptoms are making a baby unhappy and sleepless, consult with your pediatrician about giving the baby medication to lower the fever. Giving a baby a bath in tepid (not cool) water can also lower the fever temporarily. Never use rubbing alcohol to try to lower a baby's temperature. Rubbing alcohol can be absorbed into the bloodstream and cause breathing difficulties, seizures, and other health problems. Never give aspirin to children under the age of twelve—in children, aspirin has the potential to cause a rare but potentially fatal disorder called Reye's syndrome.

If a baby's temperature spikes (suddenly soaring to 105 degrees Fahrenheit, for example) he may be at risk of a febrile seizure. Febrile seizures can also be caused by lesser fevers. These seizures are usually not harmful in and of themselves, but they are frightening for parents. A baby suffering a seizure may breathe heavily, turn blue, roll his eyes back, drool profusely, and have uncontrollably shaking limbs. **If your baby has a seizure, roll him on his side. Do not put anything in the baby's mouth.** Try to make note of how long the seizure lasts (generally anywhere between ten seconds and four minutes). **After the seizure subsides, contact your pediatrician immediately, head to the emergency room, or call 911.**

Many fevers are accompanied by familiar symptoms of viral or bacterial infections—such as a runny nose, vomiting, diarrhea, or a cough. Some viral infections, such as roseola, can cause a very high fever over a three-day period, after which a light rash appears on the trunk. Other infections, including meningitis, may cause a high fever and no other symptoms. **If your baby has a high fever and no other symptoms, call your pediatrician. If your baby has a high fever or other symptoms—including extreme irritability—that suggest a serious problem, call your pediatrician and head for an ER.**

 BABY ALERT: You should call the pediatrician about any fever that your baby has in the first two to three months, and particularly in the first six weeks. Once your baby is three months old, call your pediatrician about any fever that is over 101 degrees Fahrenheit (measured rectally).

As Your Child Grows

As children get older and experience fevers, be sure they stay hydrated: water, soup, Popsicles, and flavored gelatin are all healthy options. Let your child eat whatever sounds good to him (within reason), and don't force a sick child to eat. Kids can head back to school or day care after the temperature has been back to normal for a full twenty-four hours.

Food Allergies

Avoiding the Problem

When a baby (or any of us) has an allergic reaction to a particular food, the reaction is the body's launching of an immune system defense against something it mistakes for a harmful, invading substance. Once the immune system identifies any substance as foreign to the body, it develops antibodies designed to combat that substance in the future. The next time a child ingests the substance, the body's immune system may go into high gear, releasing histamine and other chemicals to protect itself against what it thinks is harmful. In an allergic reaction, the respiratory, gastrointestinal, and cardiovascular systems, as well as the skin, can all be affected.

Food allergies are increasingly common among American children. Young children are most commonly allergic to milk, soy, peanuts (actually a legume, not a nut), tree nuts, eggs, fish, shellfish, and wheat. These food groups make up the vast majority of food allergies in children and adults, although a person can potentially be allergic to any food or substance. Ask your pediatrician about the difference between a true food allergy and lactose intolerance.

Most experts recommend breastfeeding babies until they are six months to a year old, if possible. Breastfed infants generally have far fewer allergies and fewer digestive problems.

However, even if your baby is breastfeeding she may have allergic reactions to the foods that you eat, since they show up in your breast milk. If you know of serious food allergies in your family, avoid those foods while you are breastfeeding (for example, if you or your baby's father is allergic to nuts, you should avoid eating nuts while you're breastfeeding). If you notice that your baby has a mild allergic reaction after you've eaten particular foods, try cutting those foods out of your diet and see if the trouble goes away. On the other hand, a child can have trouble digesting certain foods, causing gas and discomfort, but this is not necessarily an allergic reaction.

If you've identified foods to which your child is allergic, you'll naturally want to make every effort to avoid exposing your child to the foods or substances, even in the smallest amounts. If your child has experienced a severe allergic reaction, keep an injection of epinephrine (to be prescribed by your doctor) handy at all times. Learn how (and teach other caregivers how) to inject the epinephrine correctly.

Everyone who cares for your child needs to be aware of the food allergy: day-care employees, school staff, and friends' parents. Depending on the age of the child, you should consider getting your child an allergy bracelet, identifying the type of allergen adults need to be aware of.

Mild allergic reactions include itchiness, tingling of the lips or tongue, red or slightly swollen skin, itchy eyes, runny nose, and hives (red bumps that resemble insect bites, but are usually larger) that appear anywhere on the child's body. Call your pediatrician right away if your child has any abnormal reaction to a particular food or a change in diet.

PARENT SMART: It can be hard to tell if an infant has a true allergy to milk or a lactose intolerance. Ask your pediatrician for guidance.

What to Do if Your Baby Has an Allergic Reaction

If your child is exhibiting any of the symptoms of a severe allergic reaction, or anaphylactic shock, seek immediate medical help by calling 911. This is a life-threatening emergency.

Signs of severe allergic reaction include:

- Wheezing or difficulty breathing

- Dizziness or loss of consciousness

- Difficulty speaking or swallowing

- Swelling of face, mouth, or throat

- Abdominal pain, nausea, and/or vomiting

If your child has been exposed to a food that has caused a severe allergic reaction in the past, seek emergency medical help regardless of symptoms.

As Your Child Grows

Most milk allergies fade in time, but other allergies—such as sensitivity to nuts and shellfish—do not. As your child eats more often at school, friends' houses, and restaurants, make sure caregivers and supervising adults are aware of your child's allergies. Arm your child with information about how to avoid foods to which he or she might be allergic.

Also consider having younger children wear an ID bracelet or necklace describing the allergy, and keep Benadryl (or a prescribed epinephrine injection, depending on the severity and type of allergic reaction) handy in case an allergic reaction occurs. Consult your pediatrician to determine when to give a child Benadryl, and when it might be inappropriate, and the appropriate dosage.

BABY ALERT: Although one poll conducted by *The Wall Street Journal* found that 38 percent of parents had either given Benadryl to their children to get them to sleep on a flight, or thought about doing it, pediatricians strongly discourage this practice. Medicines should only be used for their intended purpose. Benadryl, in fact, may have the opposite effect on some children, causing them to be hyper rather than sleepy.

Foreign Objects in Ear

Avoiding the Problem

This is most commonly a problem for children who are between two and four years old, but it can happen as soon as babies have the motor skills to pick up and place things in their ears.

Items commonly inserted in the ear canal can include pieces of food, insects, small toy pieces, buttons, small batteries, and fragments of crayon. Boredom and curiosity usually lead children to place things in their ears or nose (see the following section). Some children may even stick things in the ear to alleviate the discomfort of an earache.

 PARENT SMART: Because children are obsessive imitators of adult behavior, avoid cleaning your ears with cotton swabs in front of children, since children can do serious harm to their ear canal in imitating this behavior.

For children under three years of age, the best prevention is to keep small objects (which are also choking hazards) away from children.

What to Do if Your Baby Has a Foreign Object in the Ear

Any foreign object lodged in the ear canal will require a trip to the emergency room. However, in some cases, it may not be immediately apparent that anything is lodged in the ear canal—unless it is causing diminished hearing, redness, or drainage. If you notice any of these symptoms or suspect that something has become lodged in the ear canal, make the earliest possible appointment to see your pediatrician.

Do not attempt to remove any objects lodged in the ear canal yourself—this causes more accidental ear-canal injuries than the original problem does. Well-meaning attempts to remove objects from the ear canal can result in objects being pushed deeper into the ear—resulting in a far more unpleasant and complicated problem and removal procedure for the child. It's also important to have your doctor check the ear canal after the object has been removed to make sure that no damage has been done to the internal structures of the ear.

Only infrequently will sedation be required to remove objects from the ear canal. If a child injures his ear canal by inserting an object that doesn't get stuck (such as a cotton swab), you should make an immediate appointment to see the pediatrician. Antibiotics and other treatments may be necessary to help the ear to heal properly.

As Your Child Grows

As children get older, make sure they understand that the ear is a fragile thing! They should never try to clean inside their ears on their own. Also, you should protect kids' ears by disallowing overly loud music, television, or video games.

Foreign Objects in Nose

Avoiding the Problem

As is the case with odd objects inserted in the ear (see the previous section), children usually insert things in the nose out of boredom or curiosity, or in an act of imitation. Foreign objects commonly found in children's noses include pieces of toys, tissue, and erasers. Children may even inhale foreign objects accidentally when trying to smell something too closely.

 BABY ALERT: A foreign object in a child's nose is more serious than one in the ear. It can be pushed back into the child's posterior pharynx (the back of the throat) and cause a life-threatening obstruction of the airway.

The best defense against this problem (as well as the issues of choking and small objects in the ear) is to keep small objects out of the child's reach at all times. Anything small enough to fit in the ear, nose, or airway should be kept well away from babies and young children. In addition, be careful, as always, not to do potentially dangerous things in front of babies and children (such as inhaling nose spray) that might inspire them to try emulating you.

What to Do if Your Baby Has a Foreign Object in the Nose

As is the case with objects in the ear, it may not be apparent at first that something is lodged in the nose. The most easily recognized symptom is draining of the nose—usually appearing only on the side blocked by the foreign object. The drainage may have a bad odor, and the foreign object may also cause the nose to bleed from the affected side.

If you notice any of these symptoms, or you suspect that your child has something lodged in the nose, call your pediatrician immediately. Do not attempt to remove any object from the nose yourself—this will invariably cause distress in the child, and it can lead to the need for more complicated removal procedures if the object gets pushed deeper into the nasal passage. Your pediatrician may remove the object him- or herself, but more likely the procedure will have to be done at the hospital.

As Your Child Grows

As children get older, what goes into the nose is less of a problem, but rather what comes out of it. Your baby will not be able to blow his nose until he is between three and four. Until then, you will rely on a bulb syringe to clear out mucus. Your toddler will have to be taught to blow his nose; try using a directive such as, "Pretend that you are blowing out your birthday candles, but blow through your nose."

Frostbite

Avoiding the Problem

Frostbite damages skin and tissues when ice crystals form after prolonged exposure to freezing temperatures. In cold weather, frostbite can quickly affect the extremities—fingers, toes, ears, nose, cheeks, hands, and feet as well as the face. While any of us is susceptible to frostbite, babies and children are at much greater risk of developing it. Babies lose body heat more quickly than adults do, and they can't let us know when their fingers and toes are getting too cold.

During cold winter months, dress babies warmly in multiple layers when you'll be spending time outside. Take extra care to make sure ears, fingers, and toes are all covered by warm clothing. Make sure that your child's face is protected if there will be prolonged exposure to cold. If clothing items get wet (socks and mittens in particular), be sure to replace them with warm, dry items as quickly as possible. Naturally, the most important precaution is to avoid lengthy exposure to cold weather, especially on windy days.

What to Do if Your Baby Has Frostbite

Frostnip usually precedes frostbite and is characterized by redness of the skin, a tingling sensation, and numbness.

BABY ALERT: Don't massage skin or limbs if you suspect frostnip, as this can do more damage to skin and tissues.

Symptoms of frostbite include:

- Reddened skin that turns waxy, white, hard, and swollen

- Burning sensation, tingling, or numbness of skin

- Blisters and ulcers (in the case of severe frostbite)

Left untreated, frostbite can cause the death of underlying tissues and lead to gangrene.

In the case of frostnip, warm the affected body parts gradually by using your own body heat (holding a baby's fingers in your armpits, for instance) and/or immersing the affected body part in warm water (not hot water). Do not use heating pads, warmth from a fire, or any other sources of direct heat. If warming the affected area does not help, call your pediatrician immediately.

If you suspect frostbite, call 911, stay calm, and wrap your baby in a warm blanket. If you are more than two and a half hours from an ER, immerse the affected area in warm water (104° to 108°), *not hot water.* Be careful not to let the area refreeze.

 BABY ALERT: Be especially careful not to let skin refreeze after you have warmed it—refreezing can cause severe damage to skin and tissues.

As Your Baby Grows

As kids get older and devote time to outdoor play in winter, they are more at risk for frostbite. Children who love the snow and don't want to come inside are particularly susceptible, since the combination of damp clothes, exertion, and cold can be a dangerous one. Make sure older kids know the warning signs and come inside to warm up whenever they get too cold. Check your child's internal temperature with a thermometer to identify hypothermia.

Head or Neck Injury

Avoiding the Problem

Most head and neck injuries occur as the result of a fall. If your baby is starting to walk, make sure that your home is "baby proofed." You'll want to make sure that safety gates (approved by the U.S. Consumer Product Safety Commission) are blocking all stairways and that all sharp corners on furniture are cushioned. Even if your home is baby proofed, never leave your baby alone, even for a minute. If you must answer the phone or the door, take your baby with you. If you must do household chores, wear your baby in a sling or carrier, or place your baby in a safe place within your sight, such as a playpen or baby seat. Be sure to take all common-sense precautions, such as buckling seat belts and checking to make sure the playpen sides are fully locked. See "Drops and Falls" for more precautions.

What to Do if Your Child's Head or Neck Is Injured

Most often, children will sustain only an injury to the scalp, which, can result in a lot of bleeding and a "goose egg," or swelling. Even though this is not usually serious, for children under two years of age you should consider speaking with a doctor or going to the ER. If a child is under three months of age, even a minor fall can be serious. At this age the skull is very thin and easily fractured. **If your child's wound looks serious to you, don't hesitate to get**

immediate medical help. A blow to the head can appear minor and be significant in a small percentage of children. This is more often true for younger children under age 2.

Signs of a serious injury include unconsciousness; confusion; abnormal breathing; bleeding or clear fluid coming from the nose, ear, or mouth; disturbed speech or vision; dizziness; a seizure; and vomiting more than twice. Signs of a concussion, a type of internal head injury causing a temporary loss of normal brain functioning, can include nausea and vomiting, headaches, memory loss (e.g., repeating the same question over and over), blurred vision or light sensitivity, slurred speech or speech that doesn't make sense, difficulty concentrating or thinking, anxiety, irritability, and excessive tiredness without apparent reason.

If your child does not have serious symptoms and is behaving normally, apply an ice pack, wrapped in a clean washcloth or towel, to the injured area for about twenty minutes. Observe your child carefully for the next twenty-four hours, waking him every two hours to see if his condition changes. If you notice any of the serious symptoms listed here, seek immediate medical help. Also seek immediate help if your child vomits more than two or three times. If the incident has occurred close to your child's naptime or bedtime, check your child frequently and note changes in skin color or breathing, or twitching limbs. If you are at all concerned, call your doctor immediately and describe what you see.

If your child is unconscious after a head injury, do not move your child, but rather call 911 for help. If your child is vomiting or has a seizure, turn your child onto her side while keeping her head and neck straight. This will help prevent choking and provide some protection for the neck and spine.

If your child shows symptoms of a significant injury, try to keep your child calm and still while waiting for paramedics to arrive. You can gently apply a sterile bandage if there is bleeding, but **do not attempt to clean the wound, since this may aggravate bleeding or cause complications if the skull is fractured. Do not remove any object that may be stuck in the wound, and do not apply direct pressure to the wound if you suspect that the skull may be fractured.**

As Your Child Grows

As children become more active—riding a tricycle, skateboarding, or playing sports—their chances of having a concussion grow. You can prevent most concussions by making sure that children wear proper headgear—even if they are just pedaling around on their trikes. Using proper headgear can reduce the risk of a head injury by as much as 85 percent.

PARENT ALERT: Whenever your child has a significant fall, you should take him to the ER. Neck and head injuries are very serious, but you should also be aware that one injury can mask another one. Only a physician can determine if other injuries may have occurred, especially in children under two.

Heat-Related Illnesses

Avoiding the Problem

The hot summer months present potential heat hazards for everyone, but babies and young children are especially vulnerable. If it seems uncomfortably hot to you, then you'll need to take every possible precaution to keep a baby from becoming overheated. Dehydration, decreased intake of fluids, exertion, or prolonged exposure to the sun can all cause heatstroke. Heatstroke is a serious condition that can be fatal if left untreated.

Keep babies and young children out of direct, strong sun; make sure that rooms and cars are always well-ventilated and cool. When you're going to be outside for a while, find cool, shady spots for you and your baby. Make sure strollers have sunshades that keep babies from being hit by direct sunlight while you're out and about. It's difficult to know that young babies are thirsty until they show the signs of dehydration; in hot weather, be sure to give them lots of extra fluids. Plan ahead and bring Pedialyte with you if your infant will be exposed to prolonged heat.

An extra bath in room-temperature water can help to keep your baby cool, and your baby's room should be in a cool and well-ventilated part of the house, if at all possible. Avoid going out during the hottest hours of the day; go for walks in the early morning or in the cool of evening.

What to Do if Your Baby Has a Heat-Related Illness

If your baby becomes listless or very irritable, call your pediatrician—this can be a sign of dehydration. If you suspect heat illness, **move the baby indoors immediately** (or to a shaded spot, if moving indoors is not an option). Remove clothing and **bathe the baby in cool (not cold) water**; you should also **fan the skin** to simulate the cooling effect of sweating. Be sure to cool the armpits and groin area, as these areas hold on to heat.

In addition to classic, sudden-onset heat problems, other issues (especially in babies) can build up over several days. Monitor diapers to make sure that the baby is not dehydrated and give her extra fluids in hot weather or when she is ill. Talk to your pediatrician about giving your baby electrolyte replacement solutions, such as Pedialyte. Do not add salt to any drinks or try to mix rehydrating drinks at home.

Heatstroke, the most severe heat illness, is a life-threatening development. Signs include:

- Elevated body temperature

- No visible sweat

- Dehydration (less urination, dark urine)

- Refusal to drink or eat

- Dry eyes and mouth

- Muscle cramps

- Lethargy or flaccid paralysis (a "floppy" appearance)

- Confusion or uncharacteristic irritability

- Sunken fontanelle (the soft spot on a baby's head)

- Vomiting

- Loss of consciousness

If you are concerned that your baby might be suffering from a heat-related problem or might be seriously dehydrated, contact your doctor immediately and/or head to the emergency room.

As Your Child Grows

As children get older, it may seem fine to leave them in the car for a minute or two while running a quick errand, but **don't do it**! A child's body temperature rises much more abruptly than an adult's, and children have a harder time regulating their body temperature. Within a few minutes, the temperature in a parked car in summer can quickly exceed 100 degrees, and heatstroke becomes a very real danger in a matter of minutes. It's important to keep cars locked at all times—kids can climb into cars and have a hard time getting out again. Make sure kids know that the trunk is completely off-limits.

Insect Bites

Avoiding the Problem

Ticks, fleas, mosquitoes, spiders, fire ants, and other insects are persistent and unavoidable facts of life, both in our homes and in the great outdoors. When out in nature, you can reduce the odds of your baby getting an insect bite by dressing her in long sleeves and pants. Experts recommend using insect repellent of the lowest possible concentration of DEET, but check with your pediatrician for specific recommendations. Insect repellent should be applied minimally and only on areas of exposed skin. Avoid the areas around the mouth and eyes, and don't apply any repellent to babies' hands (which often end up in their mouths). Once back indoors, wash away all repellent with mild soap and water. Try to keep down the insect population inside the house by cleaning out favorite insect niches—garages, wood piles, and attics should be cleared of spider webs.

What to Do if Your Baby Has Been Bitten

Although most of the time you will not know what kind of insect bit your child, you should keep some things in mind about the various types of insect bites.

Spider Bites

Wash the bitten area gently with soap and water. You may press an ice pack (you can also use a cloth dampened with cool water) over the bite to reduce swelling and to provide relief from discomfort or itching. Never apply a hot cloth or heating pad to an insect bite—this will only speed the spread of venom into the bloodstream. Most spider bites will not cause harm beyond a mild, localized reaction to the bite, but **bites by black widow or brown recluse spiders should be treated as medical emergencies. In all cases, if your baby is having an allergic reaction of any kind (see "Food Allergies"), or if a rash or infection develops after the bite, you should seek medical attention.** All bites can potentially lead to a secondary infection, and you should **consult your pediatrician or take your infant to the ER if a fever develops, if there is drainage from the site of the bite, if there is increasing redness around the bite after several days, or if your infant continues to experience discomfort.**

Ticks

Quick discovery and removal of ticks can prevent the transmission of Lyme disease, Rocky Mountain fever, and several other tick-borne diseases. If you find a tick on your baby, **remove the tick right away, making sure that the tick is pulled free from the skin intact (no part of the tick's head should stay embedded in the skin, where it can cause infection).**

The only proper method for tick removal is to **grasp the tick with fine-pointed tweezers as close as possible to the skin, and pull slowly and straight back (don't twist or bend the body of the tick as you pull)**. Do not burn the tick or slather it in petroleum jelly. **If you attempt to remove the tick and a portion of the tick remains in your child's skin, it must be removed by your child's pediatrician or an ER physician.**

To dispose of the tick, seal it in a small plastic bag and throw it in the trash. Ticks cannot survive in a sealed plastic bag, which is lacking in adequate humidity, but they can easily survive being flushed into the sewage system to feed again. It may also be beneficial to bring the tick to the ER, where it may be determined if it is the type of tick that transmits Lyme disease.

Clean the bite with soap and water and monitor the bite over the next few days. Lyme disease is most prevalent in the northeastern United States, but cases have been identified in all fifty states. A telltale skin rash often emerges around infected tick bites—the rash is typically about two inches in diameter and circular. The center of the bite may begin to clear as the outer edge of the rash expands, creating a bulls'-eye appearance. The rash can appear three to thirty days after the bite (with an average of seven to ten days). This rash can be found at sites other than the tick bite, and it usually lasts for several weeks. It is worth noting, however, that about 25 percent of the time there is no rash. Other symptoms include fatigue, fever, joint pain, and swollen lymph glands, and they may appear within weeks or years later. If your baby exhibits any of these symptoms after a tick bite, see your pediatrician or go to the local ER. Also, if you think the tick has been on your child for twenty-four to forty-eight hours, contact your pediatrician for possible treatment *even if there are no symptoms.*

Mosquitoes, Fire Ants, and Others

If you live in a region populated by fire ants, make sure that anywhere your baby sits or crawls is free of colonies. You can apply low-concentration DEET insect repellent on exposed skin to keep mosquitoes from biting. You may want to consult your pediatrician about the brand of insect repellent he or she recommends.

If your baby does end up with a bug bite, wash the area with soap and water and apply a cool cloth to alleviate the itching and discomfort. **If the bite becomes infected, or if your baby has any signs of an allergic reaction (see "Food Allergies"), seek medical attention.** Do not pop the blister caused by fire ant bites; what appears to be pus is actually dead tissue, which can easily become infected if exposed. Make sure your baby's fingernails are trimmed regularly so that she can't scratch itchy insect bites—any bite can become infected if opened. It is normal for bites on babies and young children to be more swollen initially, and they may form hard bumps that last for several weeks or months.

As Your Child Grows

Teaching children about tick and other insect bites should continue as she grows older and hopefully spends more and more time in the outdoors. You should keep a first aid kit in the car, including insect repellent wipes, ointment to treat itching, antibiotic creams, and so on. Have your child wear long sleeves, long pants, socks, and appropriate shoes to protect her from insect bites when she is going for a hike in the woods.

Lethargy

Understanding the Problem

Pronounced lethargy in infants—limp appearance, unfocused eyes, poor feeding, and generally nonresponsive behavior—can be a sign of infection, dehydration, or other illness. Lethargy can also indicate nutrients that are lacking or imbalanced in the body, such as sodium or potassium. In newborns, lethargy can be a sign of serious viral or bacterial infection.

What to Do in the Case of Lethargy

If a baby shows sudden lethargy or paralysis, call 911 or head immediately to the emergency room.

Seek immediate medical attention if your child is lethargic, particularly if he has a high fever.

As Your Child Grows

Meningitis is an inflammation of the membranes that surround the brain or the spinal cord. Meningitis is a potentially life-threatening condition. Although symptoms in infants are usually nonspecific, symptoms in older children can include headache, fever, stiff neck, light sensitivity, and petechia lesions. Petechia lesions are small (or occasionally large) red or purple spots on the skin that don't lose their color if you press down on them. The highest incidence of meningitis is between birth and two, but meningitis in older children can spread quickly in places where children are living in close contact, like dorms and camps. Vaccines exist for certain kinds of meningitis, so make sure your child's vaccinations are up-to-date.

The main thing that parents can do is to be aware of the symptoms of meningitis, especially when there is an outbreak in the community. Always err on the side of caution and take your child to a doctor if you are concerned about symptoms. Do not hesitate to seek help—meningitis can spread quickly and cause significant body damage as well as death, so getting prompt medical attention is of the utmost importance.

Nosebleeds

Avoiding the Problem

Nosebleeds, while scary for parents and children, are rarely an indication of anything serious. Children often suffer nosebleeds at night; it's not unusual to see a significant amount of blood on the pillow the next morning.

To prevent recurrent nosebleeds, keep the nasal lining well-moisturized with a bit of Vaseline or lanolin ointment (just inside the nose, gently with your finger). Keep the baby's room at the right humidity with a vaporizer in the room to keep air moist.

Frequent nosebleeds should be evaluated by your pediatrician. There's the remote possibility of poor blood clotting, and your pediatrician may check for this. Nosebleeds in combination with bruising, bloody gums, or poor clotting should be checked out immediately by a pediatrician.

What to Do if Your Child Has a Nosebleed

Remain calm and relaxed, so your child knows not to be worried. **While the child is seated and leaning forward (but not lying down), gently pinch the nose closed with your fingers or a cloth. Hold the nose closed for ten minutes—do not let up pressure during the ten minutes to check if the bleeding has stopped.** After ten minutes, if the bleeding has stopped, don't let the child touch or pick his nose; if he is old enough to understand, have him breathe through his mouth to avoid sneezing and thereby causing the nosebleed to start up again. If the bleeding has not stopped, apply pressure again for five minutes. If the bleeding has still not stopped, call your pediatrician.

If your child has a nosebleed in combination with a severe headache or is otherwise acting unwell, head to the emergency room. Nosebleeds accompanied by bleeding gums, bloody urine or stools, or unusual bruising are cause for concern—so call your doctor right away or head to the emergency room.

It is not uncommon for children to swallow blood when they have a nosebleed. This may cause children to cough up or vomit blood, which is normal and not a cause for additional concern.

If the nosebleeds start after your child starts a new medication, call your pediatrician.

As Your Child Grows

Nosebleeds can be caused by excessive dryness in the nasal passage, sinus infection, allergies, bacterial infection, nose picking, and foreign objects in the nose (see "Foreign Objects in Nose"). Some children are more susceptible to nosebleeds than others. In these children, the blood vessels in the nasal lining may be closer to the surface; once the nasal lining becomes irritated by nosebleeds, more nosebleeds become more likely.

Nursemaid's Elbow (Radial Head Subluxation)

Avoiding the Problem

Nursemaid's elbow is a common injury that is seen most often in children between the ages of one and three years. Usually the child has had an incident in which the extended arm was pulled. This most commonly occurs when a child falls while walking and the individual holding the hand doesn't let go. Another very common occurrence is when the child is being swung by an adult holding on to the child's hands. Occasionally, the injury occurs after an ordinary fall.

To avoid this problem, make sure that all caregivers and siblings are instructed not to swing or lift your child by the arm.

What to Do if Your Child Has Nursemaid's Elbow

If a child has nursemaid's elbow she will not use her arm and will hold the arm slightly flexed and pronated. She may have tenderness over the elbow joint (but typically no swelling), redness, warmth, or abrasions. **If your child has any of these symptoms, call your pediatrician.**

Correction of this problem is usually quick and simple, but it must be done by a physician. While supporting the radial head, the forearm is supinated or pronated and flexed at the same time. A "click" will be heard or felt.

After this procedure the child will immediately use the arm. Although the problem is fixed immediately, it may take the child a few minutes to realize that she can move her arm without pain. (We usually ask the parent to get the child to reach for something, to help the child understand that the problem is fixed.) There is no need to immobilize the arm and medication for pain is rarely necessary. Unless the child doesn't start to use the arm again soon afterward, follow-up is unnecessary.

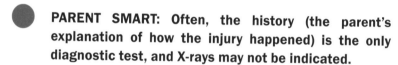

PARENT SMART: Often, the history (the parent's explanation of how the injury happened) is the only diagnostic test, and X-rays may not be indicated.

As Your Child Grows

There is a relatively high incidence of recurrence of this problem until the age of three or four. Parents should make sure that other adults are aware of this problem, and care should be taken not to repeat this injury by swinging or lifting children by the arm.

Poisoning

Avoiding the Problem

Today's homes are filled with products that are useful but also highly toxic. In fact, ordinary household products cause the majority of accidental poisonings in babies and young children. Most poisonings take place while the product is in use by a caregiver—a baby can ingest a household cleaning agent, adult medication, or baby oil in the seconds it takes a caregiver to answer the phone or to see who's at the door. Whenever a potentially toxic product is in use, a baby should not be left unobserved for even a second. If you must rush to the phone, take the baby with you.

Before you bring your baby home from the hospital, be sure to "poison proof" the house. Babies and young children are incredibly tenacious in their explorations of the world within their reach. Poisoning is a common baby emergency, in part because babies and very young children instinctively investigate objects by putting them in their mouths.

The following are some tips for poison proofing your home:

- Put all potentially poisonous substances well out of your baby's reach—including items like vitamins, baby oil, and household plants. Make a sweep of your house, removing and relocating all possibly dangerous substances to safety zones—storage areas well out of the reach of children, with doors that are kept locked.

Babies will find ways to reach higher and higher, often much earlier than parents expect. Each year, doctors handle thousands of cases of children who have managed to reach high cabinets by climbing on chairs or using other means to access cupboards theoretically out of reach.

- The American Association of Poison Control Centers (AAPCC, www.aapcc.org) provides lists of common pediatric exposures. This organization is also a good source of information regarding identification of potentially harmful substances in the home (some of the most dangerous include medications such as iron pills and over-the-counter pain and cold medicines, corrosive cleaning agents, antifreeze, paint thinner, lighter fluid, pesticides, and household plants—especially philodendron—and wild plants).

- Use, but do not rely upon, child-resistant caps for bottles. No container is truly childproof, and even very young children can outwit the manufacturer's best efforts and open bottles within a few seconds.

- Make sure all products are in their original containers and are clearly marked. In the case of an accidental poisoning, the information on the container can be crucial to proper treatment.

- Make sure children understand that *all* medicines are off-limits and serious (even sugary cough syrups). Never refer to medicines as "candy" or "treats." Do not take medications in front of children.

- Always keep your purse, bag, or diaper bag out of reach; be just as careful about where visitors leave their belongings—make sure all bags are inaccessible to babies and children.

- In the past, doctors recommended that parents keep ipecac syrup in the house to induce vomiting in children who had swallowed particular toxic substances—this is no longer the case. Evidence suggests that vomiting rarely helps and can actually do harm—it may increase the damage done by corrosive agents and may reduce the efficacy of certain emergency room treatments. In case of poisoning, do not induce vomiting.

- Post all emergency phone numbers near your phone, including the number of the AAPCC: 800-222-1222.

PARENT SMART: Grandma's handbag (or a houseguest's suitcase) is an often-overlooked source of danger for small children. ER doctors say that all too often they treat toddlers who have ingested medication found in their grandmothers' purses.

What to Do if Your Baby Has Been Poisoned

If the child has become unresponsive, has stopped breathing, or is having a seizure, call 911 immediately. If your child has stopped breathing, refer to the fold-out CPR guide for instructions on what to do while waiting for help to arrive.

If your child is conscious and breathing, call the American Association of Poison Control Centers (800-222-1222), or a local poison control number, at the first indication that your child has been poisoned.

When you call the AAPCC, you will be asked to describe your baby's condition, the substance ingested, how much of the poison was ingested, when the poisoning occurred, and the age and weight of your baby. If at all possible, you should also have the product container or bottle of the poisonous substance on hand. Your call will be redirected to a local poison control center, staffed twenty-four hours a day with doctors, nurses, and pharmacists who are knowledgeable about the best responses to an array of poisons.

Most poisonings do not evolve into crisis and can be treated at home with the guidance of experts at your local poison control center. However, if you do go to the ER, bring the bottle or label from the substance you suspect your child has ingested.

As Your Child Grows

You can further "poison proof" your home by using gentler, natural cleaning products. Whenever you can find less-toxic alternatives (such as vinegar, borax, or mineral oil) to powerful, corrosive chemicals, use them. However, continue to keep them out of reach and locked away; these may be less toxic, but they are still a danger.

Continue to educate your child about the dangers of ingesting toxic substances as he grows older. Many children experiment with household items as a way to get high. These can cause serious injury and even death.

Rash

Understanding the Problem

Although the most common rash in babyhood is a diaper rash (see "Diaper Rash"), babies are susceptible to a range of rashes as they pass through the first couple of years. Most rashes are not cause for great concern, but rashes can be a sign of serious problems.

Yeast can infect and exacerbate diaper rashes, and yeast can cause thrush in the mouth. Yeast infections on a baby's skin may be fringed by small red bumps—call your pediatrician if you suspect a yeast infection. Exposure to heat can also cause a rash, when sweat pores are blocked. Heat rash usually appears as small red bumps or blisters in infants. Mother's hormones, which remain in the baby's bloodstream for the first few weeks of life, can cause baby acne, and other rashes are common during those early weeks as well. Milia/miliaria is made up of very small white, red, or clear bumps (primarily on the face and chest), and erythema toxicum—red blotches featuring a central pimple-like bump—are common in newborns. Cradle cap appears as oily, crusty patches on the scalp, usually in the first three months.

Hives are itchy welts, red or darker than skin color, that appear and disappear as they migrate around the body. They may be most often caused by a virus or allergic reaction, and medications can cause them too.

Another common cause of rashes is eczema, a skin condition that causes patches of dry, itchy skin that is darker than normal skin color. The affected areas of the skin can thicken over time. Eczema can run in families and be associated with allergies and asthma.

Rashes can be indicative of a significant systemic illness, so always consult your pediatrician if you are concerned about a rash or skin discoloration.

What to Do if Your Baby Has a Rash

If a baby develops any kind of heat rash, move her to a cooler, less humid environment. Avoid using powders to soothe rashes, as these are easy for babies to inhale. Petroleum-based products and other ointments are more likely to trap heat by blocking pores and should also be avoided. Most rashes will disappear on their own within a few days and do not need to be treated in any way.

In the case of baby acne, use water and gentle baby soap to clean the affected area when you bathe the baby. Do not use acne medications intended for adolescents or adults. The acne will clear on its own in a few weeks.

Keep the baby's fingernails trimmed— a baby can further irritate sensitive skin by scratching. In the case of eczema, consult with your pediatrician for the best treatments—in general, it's important to keep skin from becoming too dry and dress your baby in loose, breathable fabrics that absorb perspiration (rather than trapping it against the skin). Also pay attention to foods and environmental factors that might cause an allergic reaction in your child.

Cradle cap can be treated by washing with a gentle baby shampoo; it goes away on its own eventually. If cradle cap is tenacious or becomes infected, contact your pediatrician.

If your baby develops hives, contact your pediatrician, who can try to isolate the underlying cause. He or she may prescribe antihistamines to reduce the discomfort and itchiness of hives.

Other reasons to call your pediatrician:

- Diaper rash that spreads out of the diaper area

- Rash that does not respond to home treatments after three days

- Any rash, discoloration, spots, or blisters in babies under three months

- Any rash that becomes infected

- A rash that is accompanied by other symptoms of illness, such as fever, listlessness, or vomiting

- Petechia lesions (usually small, but occasionally large red or purple spots on the skin that don't lose their color if you press down on them). Ask your pediatrician to show you a picture of this serious rash.

Infantile eczema appears as areas of skin that ooze and crust over, usually on the face and scalp. Infantile eczema can be caused by allergies, inherited sensitivities, or other genetic defects that are less understood. As babies scratch at irritated skin, the condition can worsen. Affected skin, left untreated, can become infected and be cause for concern. Symptoms may appear as part of an allergic reaction to food, certain fabrics, or hot or cold temperatures. Breastfeeding throughout the first six months may help to prevent infantile eczema.

As Your Child Grows

Most rashes, including some cases of eczema, will clear up as children get older. Consult your pediatrician whenever you see an unexplained or unusual rash.

Reaction to Shots

Understanding the Problem

Immunizations are a vitally important part of a baby's healthy development. Though babies and children can have mild reactions to vaccines, serious reactions are rare. The risk of formerly common childhood diseases without vaccination is much higher and potentially much more serious than the reaction to the shot. Immunizations for hepatitis B, DTaP (diphtheria, tetanus, and pertussis, or whooping cough), meningitis, pneumonia, mumps, measles, rubella, and chicken pox are all given in the first few months of a child's life.

A vaccine is made up of weak or dead versions of bacteria and viruses that cause a specific disease. The body's immune system mounts a defense when vaccines enter the body, and antibodies are produced and remain in the body—so that if your child is exposed to the disease in the future, the body will have the antibodies with which to better fight the infection.

What to Do if Your Child Has a Reaction to a Shot

Mild reactions to shots are common in the days following a vaccination and may include the following:

- Swelling or irritation at the site of the injection

- Mild rash that goes away in a few days

- Mild fever

Extra attention and care in the days after an immunization can ease some of the discomfort and unhappiness that sometimes come in the wake of an immunization. Make sure your baby drinks plenty of fluids after an immunization to keep from becoming dehydrated.

Most redness around the immunization site is likely to be an inflammatory response; however, anytime the skin is penetrated, a secondary infection can occur and may show up twelve to forty-eight hours after the injection. Signs of an infection can include redness, fever, and drainage. If you have any concern, call your pediatrician.

Severe reactions (within minutes or hours of vaccination) may include the following:

- Pallor

- Racing or erratic heartbeat

- Hives

- Wheezing or difficulty breathing

- Weakness

- Fainting

- Lethargy

- High fever

- Seizures

- Inconsolable, unusual crying for several minutes after the injection

In the case of a severe reaction to an immunization, you should seek immediate medical attention for your child. High fever within six weeks of the vaccination may be a reaction to vaccine (although it is more likely to be caused by another illness). Call your pediatrician if your child has a high fever.

As Your Child Grows

If your child has ever had a bad reaction to a shot or antibiotics, let your pediatrician know this before future vaccinations of any kind. Let your pediatrician know if your child has any other allergies; children with allergies to eggs or yeast, for instance, may have to avoid certain vaccines. Also, let your pediatrician know if your child has recently been ill—this may cause the doctor to delay some vaccinations.

Seizures

Understanding the Problem

There are many types of seizures. As many as 50 percent of seizures seen in emergency rooms are from an unknown cause. Seizures may be triggered by infection, high fever, head trauma, hypoglycemia, electrolyte disorder, or a neurological disorder such as epilepsy. Seizures are thought to be more common in children with autism.

In toddlers and young children, seizures can appear in the form of temporary loss of consciousness, convulsions, odd movements,

or "spacing out." Epilepsy affects over three hundred thousand children under fourteen years old in the United States. Once diagnosed, it can be managed well with anticonvulsant medications.

What to Do if Your Child Has a Seizure

Do not place anything in the child's mouth. Roll the child onto his or her side to prevent choking on saliva or vomit. Call 911 immediately.

Other behaviors that may indicate seizure in babies or young children:

- Blackouts that look like sudden, quick episodes of daydreaming

- Clumsiness or frequent falls

- Repeated action like nodding or rapid blinking

- In infants, clusters of odd movements, such as "jackknife" movements in sitting babies

- Sudden, unexplained waves of fear

- Repeated, unusual movements or twitching that can last from a few seconds to several minutes

It can be hard to identify seizures in newborns, but unusual jerking motions, disruptions in breathing, chewing movements, and erratic eye movements may be identified by a doctor as signs of seizure. If a limb is trembling due to seizure, it will continue to tremble even while it is being held. Seizures in newborns can be triggered by a variety of causes, some very serious. **If you suspect that your newborn has had a seizure, head to the emergency room.**

As Your Child Grows

Because head trauma is a common cause of seizure disorders, including epilepsy, be sure kids always wear helmets when riding bikes or scooters.

If your child is diagnosed with epilepsy, you should know that treatment advances are made every year. Visit the Epilepsy Foundation online (www.epilepsyfoundation.org) to get fact sheets and to find online-community support.

Splinters

Avoiding the Problem

Babies love to explore and the chance that they will encounter splinters is high. The most common sources of splinters are decks, wooden playground equipment, and toys made of wood. Even wooden floors may have a rough area or two. Hand-me-down cribs, which were manufactured before current safety standards were enacted, may also contain splinters.

Of course, splinters are only one of the hazards you should watch for before you put your baby down in a playground or a friend's house to wander or play. Inspect the area for sharp edges, flaking paint, and small objects.

What to Do if Your Baby Has a Splinter

Most splinters can be easily removed. Begin by washing the surface of the skin with an antiseptic such as Betadine or alcohol. If the splinter is a larger one and sticks out from the skin's surface, use a pair of tweezers (first cleaned in rubbing alcohol) to pull the splinter out.

If the splinter is too far underneath the skin's surface to be removed with tweezers, use a small needle cleaned in alcohol to move the splinter up to the surface, and then remove it with clean tweezers. After the splinter has been removed, clean the skin with soap and water. There may be a little bit of bleeding, which can be covered with an adhesive bandage.

If the splinter site is extremely painful and appears infected, if you can't remove the splinter, or if part of it is still embedded in the skin, you should take your child to see a doctor. Tetanus spores usually enter the body through puncture wounds, but it can also enter through minor injuries such as cuts and splinters. Your doctor may recommend a tetanus booster after removing the splinter. Ask the doctor about it if he or she doesn't mention a booster.

As Your Child Grows

Splinters are common when children are active, so teach your child about which areas are more likely to result in splinters, such as decks, old wooden playgrounds, or even old toys. Your older child will also be likely to get splinters when you are not around. Teach your child that splinters need to be removed the right way, with clean tweezers and soap and water, and that this should be done by the school nurse, supervising parent, or an older, experienced babysitter.

Stroller Accidents

Avoiding the Problem

Getting out of the house for a stroll can be fun and invigorating for adults and children. Both casual afternoon strolls and more-purpose-oriented outings like errands can provide important opportunities for children to take in new sights, sounds, and experiences. Strollers are everywhere these days, and most parents use them from the time their children are newborns through the early years of childhood. As a result, stroller accidents occur more often than parents might imagine. However, they are very easily prevented by keeping in mind a few basic rules:

- Do not leave a child unattended in a stroller—ever.

- Strap children in carefully and thoroughly (even for very short trips), but remember that straps and belts and other forms of restraint can cause their own danger if not used appropriately.

- Make sure all stroller accessories (such as bumpers) and toys are fastened securely to the stroller, so they don't fall or knock the baby while the stroller is in use.

- Always lock the wheels of the stroller before settling your child in the stroller.

- Make sure all releases, hinges, and moving parts are out of your child's reach.

- Open and close collapsible strollers at a safe distance from children.

- If you are using a twin stroller, make sure that the footrest is a single unit across the width of the stroller; the space between separate footrests can trap children's feet.

PARENT SMART: Always read manuals carefully before using any type of apparatus with your baby. There are many books and magazine articles on selecting safe equipment, and you can also ask your pediatrician about the brands that he or she recommends.

The surest way to avoid stroller accidents is to keep babies strapped in whenever they are in the stroller—even on the shortest jaunts and when the stroller is at rest. The vast majority of stroller accidents occur when babies fall out of their strollers, but accidents can also happen when strollers tip over. Try not to use the handles of the stroller for hanging grocery bags or other heavy items that could cause a stroller to tip. Much less often, babies are injured by strollers that collapse while they are in them, so be sure to use strollers that meet industry safety standards and discontinue using a stroller that is broken or potentially dangerous. Thousands of children end up in the emergency room each year after falls from strollers, mostly with injuries to the head or face; however, just by buckling kids in *every time*, you can ensure that almost all stroller accidents are prevented.

The same rules apply to using safety restraints in shopping carts, another cause of easily prevented accidents and injuries. Falls from shopping carts can result in fractures, head injuries, and internal injuries. For this reason, use shopping cart restraints properly and never, ever leave the child unattended.

What to Do if Your Baby Has a Stroller Accident

If you believe that the impact of an accident is significant, or if you are concerned that your child may have been injured, **call 911 and do not move your child until emergency personnel arrive on the scene**. Only if absolutely necessary should you move your baby while you wait for emergency help. Moving the child can increase the severity of the injury by causing damage to the spinal cord. (See "Head and Neck Injuries.")

If the baby has stopped breathing, lift his chin to open the airway. If the baby does not resume breathing, remove him carefully from the stroller. Gently place the baby on his back, keeping movement to a minimum, and lift the chin again. Follow the procedure on the fold-out CPR guide.

As Your Child Grows

Nearly every day we see older children—four, five, and older—riding in strollers. Understandably, parents find it easier to wheel their older children on long walking trips, rather than listen to their complaints. There is no set age at which a child should stop using a stroller, but there are height and weight restrictions. Read your stroller's manual as your child gets bigger to make sure that your stroller is right for his size, and that it is not presenting an unnecessary danger.

Also, consider having your child walk, even when he might rather be wheeled or carried. As you know, lack of exercise is a serious problem for children in the United States, and there is no time like the present to encourage your child to exercise his muscles.

Sudden Infant Death Syndrome (SIDS)

Understanding the Problem

There are no symptoms or warning signs for SIDS, nor are there diagnostic tests that can predict SIDS. Only a small percentage of SIDS victims have a history of breathing problems or other chronic illness. SIDS occurs more often in premature babies or babies with a low birth weight, and it occurs in babies under one year old but is most common in babies two to four months old.

Being put to sleep on their stomachs is the greatest single risk factor for SIDS in babies. In 1992 the American Academy of Pediatrics recommended that babies sleep on their backs, and since then there has been a 40 percent drop in SIDS.

There are several theories regarding why your baby may be more at risk when she sleeps on her stomach. It is thought that when an infant sleeps on her stomach more pressure is put on the jaw, which narrows the airway. Another explanation might be that sleeping on her stomach can cause an infant to rebreathe her own air, reducing oxygen levels and causing an increase in carbon dioxide.

Some scientists also believe that an abnormality in the part of the brain that controls breathing and awakening may be the cause of SIDS. Because of this abnormality, babies may fail to wake when they are breathing stale air or deprived of oxygen for other reasons.

What to Do if Your Baby Is Unresponsive

Stay calm. **If your baby is unconscious and/or not breathing—even if the baby is cold to the touch—immediately call 911 (or have someone in the home call 911) and begin CPR** (see the fold-out page at the back of this book). Follow the instructions given to you by the 911 operator.

> **PARENT SMART: Have you taken an infant CPR course since the birth of your child? If not, you should contact your local Red Cross chapter and enroll in a class. If you have a busy schedule, as most of us do, you can even host a CPR "home party" for you and other new parents, for a small fee. Although nothing can replace live training, the American Heart Association and American Academy of Pediatrics have jointly produced a home training kit called "Infant CPR Anytime."**

Safety Alert:
Decreasing the Risk of SIDS

Although SIDS cannot be predicted or prevented, there are things that can lower the risk for your baby.

- ALWAYS lay your baby on her back, not on her stomach or side.

- Your baby's crib mattress should be firm, with a fitted sheet.

- Don't allow blankets, pillows, or stuffed toys in your baby's crib, since these could end up over her head or face and obstruct her breathing.

- If you are using bumper pads on the crib, they should be thin and firm and attached tightly.

- Keep your baby's room warm enough so she can sleep without a blanket (but not so warm that she gets overheated).

- Do not allow any tobacco smoke in your home.

- Some pediatricians feel that a pacifier may help prevent SIDS for children over one month old.

- Get early and consistent prenatal care.

Other possible risk factors include:

- Baby has birth weight of less than 3.5 pounds

- Premature birth

- SIDS death in sibling

- Second or more in birth order

- Born to teenage mother

- Abuse of substances including tobacco by mother

As Your Child Grows

SIDS is a tragedy that can happen to very young children, but there are other sleep-related areas of concern as well. Snoring can be a problem with children, causing them to wake up throughout the night, and then have symptoms of sleep deprivation the next day. In an estimated 1 to 3 percent of children between the ages of one and nine years old, snoring may be symptomatic of sleep apnea or upper airway resistance syndrome. Although there is no connection between this syndrome and SIDS, it is a potentially serious condition that requires treatment. Children who are obese or have allergies are more at risk for this type of problem.

If your child is a poor sleeper for any reason, discuss this with your pediatrician. Symptoms that occur from lack of sleep, which can include irritability, depression, and hyperactivity, may be mistaken for psychological or behavioral disorders.

Sunburn

Avoiding the Problem

A baby's skin is thinner and much more sensitive than an adult's. Babies—regardless of skin tone—need protection from the sun. Babies younger than six months should be kept out of direct sunlight entirely. Also, protect your baby's eyes with child-sized UV-protective sunglasses when he is a bit older.

A sunburn can be a serious condition in infants and very young children, but it is easily prevented. In hot climates or bright sun, make sure your baby's skin is covered in light clothing—long sleeves, pants, and hats with wide brims. For skin not covered by clothing, apply a baby-safe, waterproof sunscreen with at least 15 SPF; use sunscreen sparingly on the face and hands (to keep your baby from ingesting sunscreen). Consult with your pediatrician regarding sunscreens that are safe for babies under six months old. Keep your baby well hydrated with plenty of fluid. While breast milk or formula is best for young babies, any liquid the baby will take is okay. The important thing is to keep your child well hydrated. In hot climates or intense summer months, try to stay out of the sun completely between ten in the morning and three in the afternoon.

What to Do if Your Baby Has a Sunburn

If your baby has a mild sunburn, place a cool, damp cloth over the sunburned area for ten minutes a few times a day (taking care not to let the baby get a chill). Don't use petroleum-based products on sunburn, as these can trap heat and sweat and exacerbate sunburn. Use water-based moisturizer instead. If a sunburn is itchy and peeling, calamine lotion may relieve some of the discomfort. Keep your baby out of the sun when his skin is peeling or when he is recovering from a sunburn.

If the baby develops a fever or is in pain, or if you are concerned for other reasons, call your pediatrician. Ask him or her about the appropriate amount and type of Tylenol to give your infant.

If the skin blisters within the first twenty-four hours of the burn, arrange to see your pediatrician. Don't cover or pop blisters; this can make the sunburn susceptible to infection. If the baby loses consciousness or vomits, or if you suspect heat-related problems (see "Heat-Related Illnesses"), head to the emergency room.

If a baby under a year old gets a severe sunburn, call your pediatrician right away—a severe sunburn can become a medical emergency. Call your pediatrician if the sunburn is accompanied by fever, blisters, or pain in a baby over the age of one year.

As Your Child Grows

Keep your child well protected from the sun as he gets older and spends more time playing outdoors. This is especially important for fair-skinned children who have less natural protection against the sun's rays. Make sure kids wear sunscreen and hats and are careful to get out of the sun if they feel themselves getting burned.

There is evidence that severe sunburns and repeated exposure to the sun in childhood may increase the risk of skin cancer later in life, so always make sure that your child is wearing sunscreen and that it is applied repeatedly throughout the day.

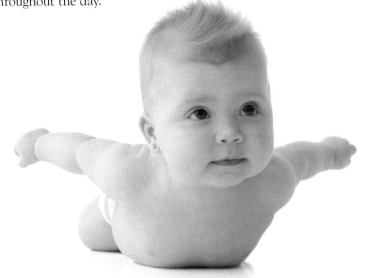

Vomiting

Understanding the Problem

There is a difference between vomiting and spitting up. Vomiting is the forceful throwing up of stomach contents through the mouth. Spitting up (most commonly seen in infants under one year of age) is the easy flow of stomach contents out of the mouth, frequently with a burp.

Vomiting occurs when the abdominal muscles and diaphragm contract vigorously while the stomach is relaxed. This reflex action is triggered by the "vomiting center" in the brain.

Unpleasant as it is to see your child be sick, vomiting is rarely anything to worry over. Vomiting is caused by a wide range of problems—most of them not serious conditions. In infants, vomiting is most often caused by:

- Overfeeding (if you're bottle feeding, make sure the nipple on the bottle is the right size)

- Motion sickness

- Excessive crying

- Acid reflux

- Gastroenteritis, an infection of the digestive tract

- Food allergies or milk intolerance

- Infection or other illness, accompanied by fever or other symptoms

- Accidental poisoning (if you suspect poisoning, head straight to the emergency room)

Babies spit up often in their first few weeks, as they get accustomed to feeding and to their environment. Vomiting (as opposed to spitting up) is the forceful expulsion of liquid; your baby may be upset by vomiting, while spitting up rarely fazes babies. If your baby is gaining weight and appears otherwise happy and healthy, vomiting is not cause for concern.

What to Do if Your Baby Vomits

If vomiting is accompanied by any of the following, you should contact your doctor or head to the emergency room:

- A swollen or tender abdomen

- Lethargy or extreme irritability

- Severe abdominal pain

- Seizures

- Strenuous, frequent vomiting or vomiting that lasts longer than twenty-four hours

- Signs of dehydration—dry mouth, few wet diapers, sunken fontanelle (soft spot on the head), and tearless crying

- Blood or green bile in the vomit (take a sample of the vomit to the doctor's office or emergency room)

- In a newborn, vomiting forcefully within thirty minutes of eating, or "projectile vomiting" (there is a chance that your baby is suffering from pyloric stenosis, a rare condition most commonly found in boys ages three to four weeks and up to eight weeks in which the muscle between the stomach and the intestine fails to open; the problem is easily corrected with surgery, but it does need immediate medical attention).

BABY ALERT: Vomiting, along with diarrhea, can rapidly lead to dehydration. Make sure that your baby is consuming normal amounts of liquid; if she refuses liquids, contact your pediatrician immediately.

As Your Child Grows

In the case of vomiting caused by normal childhood illness, comfort your child and keep her well hydrated. Ask your pediatrician for a recommendation of an electrolyte solution or give her water or diluted apple juice in small amounts every half-hour. Once the child stops vomiting, move gradually back to her regular diet.

Weight Loss

Avoiding the Problem

In the first year of life, babies grow at an amazing rate—on average, they gain ten inches in length and triple their birth weight. After the first birthday, growth slows down a bit and evens out by the second year. Each time you visit the pediatrician, your baby's height and weight will be measured. Babies who fail to meet developmental markers are described as failing to thrive. "Failure to thrive" can also describe the condition of babies who do not progress according to the developmental charts.

Regular visits to the pediatrician will allow you to be aware if your child falls below the norm on standard growth charts.

Dehydration can cause weight loss and can be serious. If your baby is underweight, looks unwell, or has sunken eyes, a sunken fontanelle (the soft spot on his head), pallor, listlessness, or extreme fussiness, you should get him immediate medical attention.

 PARENT SMART: A newborn may lose up to 10 percent of his body weight in the first few days, and this should not be a reason for concern. Your baby will regain this weight in about ten days.

What to Do if Your Baby Is Losing Weight

If you worry that your baby is losing weight, you should call your pediatrician right away so the underlying problem can be addressed. Unexplained weight loss can be caused by a range of problems, many easily resolved. If a baby is not getting enough calories, he will begin to lose weight. Poor feeding techniques or improperly mixed formula can cause weight loss in babies who are otherwise well cared for. Neglect or emotional deprivation can also cause babies to fall behind in weight gain. Gastrointestinal problems—including allergies, reflux, parasites, and chronic diarrhea—can all cause failure to thrive.

You can help your doctor out by keeping track of the following:

- How many times a day your baby is fed

- How much your baby eats at each feeding

- If breastfeeding, how long the baby spends at each breast

- Frequency, volume, and consistency of bowel movements

- Number of wet diapers a day

If there is no immediate condition that needs to be addressed, your baby's weight will be watched closely by the pediatrician. He or she may recommend that you see a lactation counselor, if you're breastfeeding, to learn how to increase breast milk production until the baby reaches six months and can branch out to other forms of nutrition.

As Your Child Grows

As children grow older and begin to expand their diets, make sure that healthy eating habits are a part of everyday life. A balanced diet rich with essential vitamins and minerals—high in whole grains and vegetables—makes kids healthy, strong, and better able to thrive in all parts of life. If your child is an extremely picky eater, he may also have trouble gaining weight at a normal rate. Do whatever you can to lessen the stress and pressure around mealtimes. Give your child lots of healthy snacking options so he can eat when he's ready to. And remember: a little juice goes a long way for children—it's easy for kids to fill up on juice and not be hungry when mealtime rolls around.

Adequate rest is essential to healthy growth, as is exercise. Most children need ten to twelve hours of sleep per night, and hearty exercise every day. Without these, a child's body cannot grow healthfully and vigorously. Obesity is an increasingly serious problem among American children, so make exercise a regular and fun part of your child's life: hiking, biking, skating, playing sports, and anything else that gets kids active.

BABY ALERT: Do not apply adult dieting principles to your child. For example, a low-fat diet that might be appropriate for a grown-up would likely have too little fat for a growing child. Ask your pediatrician for recommendations about nutrition for your child at different ages.

PART 4

appendices

Emergency Hotlines

National Emergency Hotlines

Boys Town Suicide and Crisis Line:
800-448-3000 or 800-448-1833 (TDD)

Provides short-term crisis intervention and counseling and referrals to local community resources. Counsels on parent-child conflicts, marital and family issues, suicide, pregnancy, runaway youth, physical and sexual abuse, and other issues. Operates twenty-four hours, seven days a week.

ChildHelp USA National Child Abuse Hotline:
800-4-A-CHILD (800-422-4453) or 800.2.A.CHILD (222.4453, TDD)

Provides multilingual crisis intervention and professional counseling on child abuse. Gives referrals to local social service groups offering counseling on child abuse. Operates twenty-four hours, seven days a week.

Missing & Exploited Children Hotline
1-800-843-5678

National Domestic Violence/Child Abuse/ Sexual Abuse:
800-799-SAFE or 800-799-7233 or 800-787-3224 (TDD)
800-942-6908 Spanish Speaking
Provides crisis intervention and referrals to local services and shelters for victims of partner or spousal abuse. Operates twenty-four hours, seven days a week.

National Institute of Mental Health
1-888-ANXIETY (1-888-269-4389)

National Suicide Prevention Lifeline
1-800-273-TALK

Panic Disorder Information Hotline
800-64-PANIC

American Association of Poison Control Centers
1-800-222-1222

Your Baby's Health at a Glance

Baby Medical Information

Name _____

Date of Birth _____

Pediatrician (Name and Phone) _____

_____

_____

Hospital Where Baby Was Born _____

Weight

At Birth _____ 9 Months _____

3 Months _____ 12 Months _____

6 Months _____ 18 Months _____

Known Allergies _____

_____

Vaccination History _____

_____

_____

History of Illness and Medical Care _____

_____

_____

Special Medical Conditions _____

_____

_____

Personality (for example, fussy, calm, anxious, easygoing)

_____

Parent and sibling history of medical problems

_____

_____

Your Personal Emergency Contacts

Name

Best Phone Number

Alternate Phone Number

Name

Best Phone Number

Alternate Phone Number

Name

Best Phone Number

Alternate Phone Number

Name

Best Phone Number

Alternate Phone Number

Name

Best Phone Number

Alternate Phone Number

Name

Best Phone Number

Alternate Phone Number

Name

Best Phone Number

Alternate Phone Number

If Your Infant Is Choking (for children **under 1 year**)

Caution: This guide is meant to be used as a supplement to—not a substitution for—a course in CPR and child rescue. Please enroll in an approved course today. See other important cautions on page ix.

CALL 911 IMMEDIATELY IF YOUR CHILD IS CHOKING. Do nothing if your baby is coughing, breathing, or talking. Do not hold your baby upside down or shake him.

If you suspect your baby is choking on an object—if he has an ineffective cough, is unable to move air, or is turning blue—do the following:

1. Hold your baby face down as shown. Support the infant's head and jaw with your hands, keeping your hands away from his neck.

2. Give up to 5 firm back slaps between your baby's shoulder blades with the heel of your hand. If water or vomit comes out, clear the mouth. If this does not work, go to step 3.

3. Turn your baby face up as shown. Support the back of his head with your hand and keep his head lower than his abdomen. Push on the chest 5 times using 2 fingers placed 1 finger's width below the nipple line. Push about once every second.

4. Repeat sets of back slaps and pushing the chest (steps 2 and 3), until the object comes out and your baby can breathe, cough, or cry.

If your child becomes unresponsive (and you cannot find a pulse), **follow CPR as described on the fold-out guide** and send someone to call 911. If you are alone, begin CPR for 5 cycles or 2 minutes, then call 911. After each cycle of CPR, look in the mouth, open the airway, and remove object if seen. Continue CPR until relieved by medical personnel.

If Your Child Is Choking (for children **over 1 year**)

Caution: This guide is meant to be used as a supplement to—not a substitution for—a course in CPR and child rescue. Please enroll in an approved course today. See other important cautions on page ix.

1. Ask your child: **"Are you choking?"** If your child can speak, breathe normally, or cough, call 911, sit your child in a position of comfort, and stay with your child until the ambulance arrives.

2. If he has an ineffective cough, is unable to speak or move air, has a high-pitched noise while inhaling or no noise at all, or is turning blue, your child needs intervention. **Stand behind the child with your arms wrapped around his waist.**

3. Make a fist, placing the thumb side against your child's abdomen, just above his belly button, and below the lower tip of his breast bone. Grab your fist with your other hand.

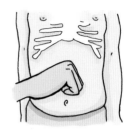

4. Pull your fist upward into your child's abdomen* with up to 5 quick, distinct thrusts. For small children, use less force.

If a child is choking while on the ground, and he is responsive, you may attempt abdominal thrusts while he is on the ground.

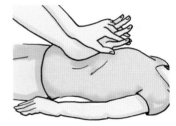

Check your child to see if the obstruction has been cleared. Each time you open the airway, look for the obstructing object in the back of the throat. Remove it if you can.

If your child stops breathing or becomes unresponsive, and you cannot find a pulse, **follow CPR as described on the fold-out guide.** Continue CPR until relieved by medical personnel.

*Note: Any child who has had abdominal thrusts or has had a significant choking event should be evaluated by a physician.

Notes